BEHIND THE SCENES

SECRETS FROM THE TOP COACHES,
EXPERTS, AND CONSULTANTS

KIM WALSH PHILLIPS

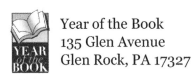

CONTENTS

FOREWORD

KIM WALSH PHILLIPS

I CAN STILL SMELL THAT AWFUL ROOM...

I had traveled to do a consulting gig and there was only one motel in town so I was stuck even though it smelled horrible, had obviously seen its fair share of illegal activity, and I was pretty sure my identity was about to be stolen by the front desk who scanned my driver's license and credit card.

As I sat on the bed, comforter off, my shoes still on because I may have to run for it at any moment, I thought to myself...

How the heck did I end up here?

Oh yeah, I needed the money.

You see, a client offered me $1,500 to do this consulting gig and I was willing to travel for three days because I was always operating out of crisis and fear. But I knew I could never put myself through this ridiculous torture again. Something *had to change.*

On my drive back up from that client, who didn't even have the check ready when I went on-site as we had previously discussed, I stopped at an association conference. On stage someone was talking about marketing and I thought to myself how much I'd love to do that.

At the end of his talk he made an offer for a digital course on marketing that cost $1,500. And people started running to the back of the room. Person, after person, after person.

I counted and there were over 100 people in line to buy his $1,500 course.

In one hour, he generated over six figures, while it had taken me the previous three days to earn just $1500.

I knew I needed to figure out how to change the way I approached my work.

Tony Robbins says, "If you want to be successful, *find someone who has achieved the results you want* and copy what they do and you'll achieve the same results."

So I started seeking experts who had done it before. I attended their events, took their courses, became a student of their success, and eventually launched my own webinar.

On my first try, I sold three courses at $1,000 each and I was thrilled. I had just earned $3,000 in one hour. That's double what it had taken me three days to earn before.

Then I kept learning, kept testing, and kept taking action.

And our sales grew.

We had our first $10,000 day. And then a $25,000 day. And finally (insert happy dance) a six-figure day.

I went from being someone who hawked her engagement ring in order to make payroll, to being named this year #475 on the Inc 5,000.

It's because I sought change... and instead of reinventing the wheel, I found experts who had achieved what I yearned for, and then used their blueprints.

The chapters that follow are your blueprints. Read their stories, take their expert advice. Crush your next goal. You are holding the answer in your hands right now.

You will hear from the following experts:

ANGEL FRANCE DUGAS, style expert and coach who teaches on how to dress to attract the clients you want without spending heaps of money.

BARBARA HARRINGTON, professional coach who teaches you how to set your goals so they move from dream to reality so you accomplish everything you intended.

BRAD ROSS, magician and influencer who has helped himself and other business owners become the authority in their niche and set them apart from the crowd.

CATHY FROST, wellness expert who teaches how dieting should no longer be a factor. Instead you can focus on your metabolism and water intake to stay in those skinny jeans forever.

CHERYL SCHINDLER, social media expert who uses information found through these platforms to close more deals and increase profits.

DANIEL SCHINDLER, shotgun shooting instructor and coach who realized skills as a coach go beyond your individual niche. Consult with those who have put in the work.

DENISE FAY, marketing guru who shares how the words you choose will attract your target clients and keep them buying from you over and over again.

DIANA ASAAD, crisis marriage counselor who helps those struggling to learn how to embrace their blocks, granting you the ability to forge deeper relationships or grow your client base.

DR. KAZ, elite performance coach who helps athletes and executives become unstuck and enables them to succeed by maximizing their impact.

DR. FRED ROUSE, bestselling author and Certified Financial Planner who teaches how to make sure you have enough in retirement savings without depending on the stock market to grow your account.

HOWARD GLOBUS, IT security expert who provides customer service solutions for small businesses via the first point of contact for many—the phone system.

JENNIFER CARMAN, parenting coach who uses humor to provide help through roadblocks and hurdles.

JON TOY, visual sign creator who shares techniques to stand out amongst your competitors when you're all fighting for the same consumers.

LOLA WHITE, wellness coach who shares how her own self-healing inspired her to teach other women to love themselves through healthy eating.

MAGDA CASTAÑEDA, Registered Nurse and coach who assists others in lowering their sugar intake to lead healthier and more fulfilling lives.

MARIE-PAULE SINYARD, kitchen design expert whose own near-death experience helps guide others to embrace fear and use it to accomplish their goals.

MIMI SHEFFER, social media coach who shares how building your brand leads to more clients and generates more revenue.

RAY MILLER, nutrition practitioner and healer who assists patients diagnose pain, often caused by internal stressors, and lead a healthier life.

DR. RUSSELL STRICKLAND, dissertation coach and adviser who counsels adults on how self-doubt and perfectionism can be redirected to get them to their goal quicker.

SUZI SEDDON, digital course maven who switched her focus at the age of 56 by forming a Facebook group to launch a digital course and monetize her audience without spending any money out of pocket.

TAMI SANTINI, destination wedding coach who learned how the power of "no" transformed her mindset, shifted her focus, and helped her capitalize on selling her knowledge to other travel agents.

DR. TERI ROUSE, educator and parental support guru whose own blended family experience helped her become an advocate for youths struggling both academically and emotionally.

VAL HEART, animal communicator who realized that better communication with animals leads to better communication with all the humans in your life.

Pick topics that align with your goals and take action.

Because there is one way to reach your final destination... taking the next step.

Claim your free gift!

GET THE BEHIND THE CURTAIN POWER PACK

Claim over $10,358 worth of bonuses, including:

- Million-Dollar Swipe file by Kim Walsh Phillips
- It's My Birthday Credit Promo by Dr. Russell Strickland
- Ultimate Relaxation recording by Jennifer Carman
- Graphics Branding Tutorial Video, Social Media Clever Caption Guide, and Social Media Timing Cheat Sheet by Mimi Sheffer
- 14 Days Without Sugar Guide by Magda Castañeda
- A review of your current phone answering and follow-up process (or create one from scratch) and work one on one to customize your process with Howard Globus
- *4 Easy Steps To Fit Into Your Skinny Jeans* digital book by Cathy Frost
- The Course Creator SuperBundle by Suzi Seddon
- The Ultimate Secure Retirement Roadmap by Dr. Fred Rouse
- $1199 worth of savings and promotions from FASTSIGNS
- 27 Headline Formulas Guaranteed to Convert by Denise Fay
- And much, much more besides!

BEHINDTHESCENESBOOK.COM/POWERPACK

MAGNETICALLY ATTRACT YOUR PERFECT CLIENT

ANGEL FRANCE DUGAS

HOW CAN YOU GROW BUSINESS AND MULTIPLY SALES by creating "Your Magnetic Brand"?

Why is it even important to have your perfect magnetic brand? Branding allows you to express to the world who you are without saying a word. Think of it as a form of silent selling. Developing your magnetic brand allows the attraction of clients and team members that you desire, plus it brings opportunities to you. When you feel and look your ultimate best, a positive posture is created. This radiating posture influences everyone who interacts with you, whether in person or on the internet.

Let's look at a few brands that we immediately recognize when we see the logo or owner.

- The Big Golden "M" Arches = McDonalds
- A fun Internet company with colorful logo = Google
- When you saw Steve Jobs in his black turtleneck = Apple
- When you see or hear the name Sophia Amoruso or #GIRLBOSS = Nasty Gal (business/movie)

I could continue naming different logos, people, and businesses, however, my goal is for you to create your own magnetic brand.

Are you dressing to attract the perfect client for the lifestyle you live each day? This would include reviewing your dreams/goals, understanding the body type you are blessed with, utilizing your specific clothing style personality. and learning to wear the colors that make you more vibrant.

You may be thinking that in order to attract the opportunities I am talking about, you will need to hire an image consultant/stylist, or some other professional. Great style is not dependent upon spending heaps of money. It's all about designing your own unique flair to represent you to those you encounter. The reality is, you can dress to create your personal brand to grow your business on any budget. It's all about designing who you are, and the process is almost the same as creating your business logo. You need to craft what you are saying about your business through the clothes you choose to wear. Branding is all about marketing you, personally.

Do you want to grow your business and attract customers who are perfect for you?

If the answer is "YES!" then imagine, if you will, that you are at a crowded event or on social media. How do you stand out to your future clients or team members? Your brand image is what makes the difference. Unfortunately, there is only a small percentage of female entrepreneurs who dress to fit their style to attract their "perfect client." Everyone else is dressing to the latest trends or what a magazine says they should wear.

As women, we have a tendency to mask ourselves behind our clothing. This masquerade of hiding happens because we were never taught how to proudly brand ourselves. Another developed tendency is we think and/or say that "I do not have the perfect body" or the "perfect look." Remember that attracting the perfect client is not about having the perfect body or the perfect look. The great thing is that you already have all you need. You just need to be you and learn how to express your perfect unique style. You are the business entrepreneur that others want to learn from and emulate, so you deserve to become the superstar in your industry by creating your magnetic brand.

Creating your brand begins with you expressing who you are and who you desire to become.

Just think, you are a celebrity, preparing to have your dress designed for you to walk on the red carpet. You probably think your designer will take your measurements first. Not true!

The first question most famous designers will ask is: "What is it that you want others to think about you... within the first three seconds of your appearance?" Wow, when I first heard this I was blown away.

In business we are initially taught the 93% rule. This was a study conducted by the University of Illinois that discovered first impressions are created in less than seven seconds. Amazingly, these first impressions that are formed in less than seven seconds are broken up into three sections:

- 55% based on appearance (your dress and grooming)
- 38% based on verbal tone (how you speak and pace)
- 7% based on verbal content (the words we speak)

Let's now talk about how we are going to begin designing your Magnetic Brand.

What is the first impression you desire?

My question to you as a professional business owner is: What is the first impression you want others to think about you when they meet you either in person, on social media, or in some other fashion online?

As a female entrepreneur, you live your red-carpet moment every day; you are the celebrity of your business and the industry you represent. People dream of wanting your lifestyle that you have designed. This is why they want to join you as a client or team member – desiring to have their heart-filled dreams come true and enjoy success as you have. You are the celebrity they admire.

So, what do you want them to think about you in their first three seconds of meeting you?

Let's talk about a few clients and what they want people to think of them in their first few seconds.

Client 1 wants everyone to know she has created the lifestyle she and her family dreamed of, which is living at the beach. So, when you see her, she dresses the part and works from her beach home. (Her daily outfits include sundresses with hats and sunglasses or shorts with a fun top.)

Client 2 sells clothing. You will see her in different outfits that are extremely fashionable. She uses my program to become more creative and mix and match her different outfits to create more combinations.

Client 3 is always sporting her latest accessories from her own jewelry company and makes sure she wears solid colors that accentuate her jewelry. Using the techniques in our program, she dresses to her body type and style, then mixes and matches her jewelry with the appropriate clothing.

Client 4 sells skin care and makeup. In that business, image is an essential part to creating an impressive brand. She knows how important it is to dress appropriately for her daily activities to attract her perfect client. Our system has guided her to dress her best styles in all situations, coordinating her clothing with her makeup to have a completed look.

Now, each one of these ladies dresses the part, and adjusts their clothing styles when they attend meetings or conventions... wearing dresses, cardigans, business suits, pants and/or evening gowns as appropriate.

What is your lifestyle and where do you see yourself in 1 year, 5 years and 10 years?

When creating your style, you should look at daily habits and ask yourself: "Where do I see myself in the future?" That is why your dream is so important. In business, you should not only look at the here and now, but you must look to the future and rediscover the dreams that are deep down in your heart. This vision allows you to design your wardrobe for both the present and future you!

The Physical YOU!

I know. When I say this I usually hear, "Oh no, not that." Yes, you need to know your current bust, waist, and hip measurements. By knowing these measurements, it allows you to move forward to the next step to discover your body type.

How to Dress for Your Body Type

Now that you know your measurements, you can begin planning your wardrobe to conceal those areas you are not excited about and accentuate your amazing features. Style recognizes no size! So, whether you wear a size 0 or 4X-plus, it does not matter! What matters is *you*, and that you learn how to dress for the perfect body type you have been blessed with.

4 body types

Unfortunately, most women have a tendency not to dress for their specific body type. Instead they hide behind their clothing, by wearing items that are boxy. This boxy presentation does not give a true expression of who they are. And this means they are not attracting that ideal client or team member.

These are the different shapes and how to tell which one you are. You can look at yourself in the mirror or use the measurements you took previously.

- Triangle – Smaller on the top (Bust and Waist), lower part of body is larger (Hips and Buttocks)
- Rectangle – Bust, Waist and Hips are all straight and pretty much even
- Hourglass – Smaller at the Waist area, Bust and Hips are about the same size
- Inverted Triangle – Smaller on the lower part of your body (Hips and Buttocks), more endowed on the top (Bust and Shoulders)

Your Clothing Style Personality

Discovering your clothing personality and dressing to fit your specific style is an important key ingredient. There are six different clothing personality styles and we usually mix a combination of two. This means there is a possible 36 combinations. That is why a friend may look better in an outfit you would love to wear, while you look better in outfits they only wish they could pull off.

A few words you might hear when people talk about you to help you determine which clothing style personality you fall into:

- *Dramatic* – Bold, Stands Out, Attention, Makes a Statement
- *Natural* – Easy-going, Relaxed, Low Maintenance, Sporty, Girl-next-door
- *Gamine* – Cute, Perky, Fun, Energetic, Optimistic
- *Classic* – The Lady, Regal, Confident, Tailored
- *Romantic* – Feminine, Passionate, Charming
- *Ingenue* – Girly-girl, Youthful, Sweet, Innocent

Cool vs. Warm

Discovering colors to wear that make you look fabulous, will have you standing out in the crowd. There are ways to determine if you are cool or warm and which of the four seasons you are (Spring, Summer, Autumn, or Winter). While there are other contributing factors to consider, here is a great tip to assist in determining if you have cool or warm undertones.

What color are your veins?

Look on the inside of both wrists to view your veins. Are they thin, not really visible and/or are they blue/purple?

If they look blue/purple, you probably have cool undertones. You will look great in pinks or black which are in the color pallets that fall into Summer or Winter.

If veins appear thicker and green/aqua in color, this suggests warm undertones will suit you. You will look great in corals and browns which are in color pallets that fall into the Spring or Autumn.

If you have difficulty determining, or if you have blue and aqua veins mixed, you probably will lean closer to neutral. You will want to look at the Spring and Summer colors. This allows you to wear a variety of colors.

Pulling it All Together

Once you have the previous steps done, it is time to create your signature look that tells the world who you are without speaking a word.

First Impression

_____

Daily Lifestyle

_____

Dream/Goal

_____

Physical You!

Bust _____

Waist _____

Hips _____

Body Type

_____

Clothing Personality

_____

Cool or Warm

_____

Your brand is your ultimate competitive advantage and I want you to stand out, attract new clients, expand your opportunities, and increase your profits. Understand that when you look good, you feel good. Your appearance is the single most important factor when it comes to attracting opportunities both socially and professionally.

If you are ready to discover how to attract new clients, without spending a dime on marketing, and know how to dress in your best styles to impress in any setting, then plan to join our upcoming workshop to discover more about Your Magnetic Brand https://yourmagnetic.com/optin

Angel France Dugas

ANGEL FRANCE DUGAS has traveled nationally and internationally as a speaker, coach, and trainer. (Fun Fact: as a child she changed clothing about 4 to 6 times a day which prepared her to share with women that they have 4 different costumes they change into on a daily basis.)

She is a wife, daughter, sister, step-mom, dancer, and knows God inspires her.

And she's obsessed with empowering women to be their very best to increase their opportunities and profits.

Angel's Superpower is to bring out the inner beauty and "WOW Factor" of women entrepreneurs in the Direct Sales/Network Marketing Industry.

H.A.R.D. GOALS
The Real Secret of Getting
from Where You Are to Where You Want to Be

BARBARA HARRINGTON

> *Dreams come a size too big so we can grow into them.*
> *—J Bissett*

FROM MY OWN EXPERIENCES, the strongest way to reach your dreams and goals is to think counter-intuitively. In observing my coaching clients, they seem to want to play small. But why? Why does it seem "crazy" or "scary" to play the bigger game?

Why don't we live the life we really *really* want?

Perhaps when we were younger we heard something like: "Dreamers are losers" or "That's just pie in the sky stuff" or "It is not polite to ask for more" or "You are just setting yourself up for disappointment." Unfortunately, after we hear these statements often enough, we begin to believe they are true. When applied to goal-setting activities, the tendency becomes to set goals one already knows how to accomplish. That's playing it small.

I grew up with the idea (and I bet you did, too) that in order to achieve your goals, you needed to also know exactly how you would do it before you even started. Furthermore, you needed to plan a logical, stepwise, linear progression. (Thank you, Newtonian Physics, wherein the Quantum Physics results can be exponential.)

If your dreams don't scare you, you aren't dreaming big enough!

I have studied goal setting for 40 years, and I truly thought I was doing the right thing by creating mine logically, and step-by-baby-step. I soon realized I would easily get bored with my goals though. I didn't finish what I started. Instead I procrastinated, and then I was just plain stuck.

I have to admit, the goals I chose weren't fun to accomplish either. I wanted to be "successful." But even though I wanted to be successful, the work wasn't fulfilling and it was impossible to get excited about it. But hey, I had this wonderful job. What was wrong with me?

So, I looked for wisdom from the late Stephen Covey. "Begin with the end in mind," he coaches in *7 Habits of Highly Successful People*. I knew that setting goals was far better than just winging it. And I knew that writing them down was also important. Recently it was pointed out to me that we are goal-seeking organisms. Without goals, we are actually lost. In fact, without a dream to work toward, we are just reacting to life and getting nowhere in the process.

For me, I had big goals and dreams. But that didn't mean I worked on them daily. I kept hearing my mental program loop saying, "That's just pie in the sky stuff, Barb! You aren't good enough or smart enough to do those things."

Do you have these conversations with yourself? Before you call me crazy, just know we all have this mechanism trying to keep us safe from harm's way. "Play it small," it says. "Be safe," it says.

Let's rephrase the question as: "How can you set your goals so you can actually accomplish your dreams?"

The setting of goals is actually the easy part. *Achieving* them is where it gets real because your brain still sees change as a threat to your existence. Yes, this is the brain's main function – keeping us safe – and change is something that threatens the brain's very being. To our brains, any change is perceived as a risk.

To stop playing small, ask yourself this set of questions:

- Why is it so hard to break thought or behavior patterns?
- Why do I start and stop things, only to be back at square zero?
- Why do I get stuck earning the same level of income?
- Why can't I complete my goals to get to the life I want?

Think of a thermostat. It is a cybernetic mechanism which keeps the temperature constant. In summer, our house warms up, and the change is registered with the thermostat which turns on the A/C to cool things down to a set temperature.

Our human minds operate much the same way with our thoughts, feelings, and behaviors. We have a comfort point, and when we are off-track, the brain kicks in to bring us back to that set "temperature."

The good news, is we can override the system and finally achieve lasting change.

To get where you want to be, you need to wake up every morning excited about working toward your goals and dreams

Most people I know set what are called *S.M.A.R.T. goals:*

- *Specific* – simple, sensible, significant
- *Measurable* – meaningful, motivating
- *Achievable* – agreed, attainable
- *Relevant* – reasonable, realistic and resourced, results-based
- *Time Bound* – time-based, time limited, time/cost limited, timely, time-sensitive

The idea is that when you set *S.M.A.R.T* goals, they are tangible, specific, and attainable. This suggests you may have a better chance of success.

The premise is that you will create incremental, linear tasks in order to reach the goal. For example, if you met your overall goal of a 5%

increase in sales, you might ask yourself to increase your sales by an additional 5% in the coming year, for a total of a 10% increase.

In my experience with this methodology, I really never pushed beyond the resources I had at hand. I definitely stayed within my limits (kind of like coloring within the lines). Those realistic, logical, and achievable goals left me stuck. Uninspired. I didn't feel challenged.

I kept thinking there had to be a better way to set goals, and to get more out of myself. No one ever taught me how to take a dream or vision and imagine it as a future outcome, as if it had already happened. But by future pacing your goal, you can allow yourself to feel the emotions as if the dream has already been achieved.

Through doing this simple activity I'll show you next, you can turn that vision into a set of activities that will take you closer to your goal every day, thereby dramatically improving yourself and what you are doing to get a better bottom-line result. Fundamentally this moves you to a whole new awareness.

Future pacing – Permission to dream

Take out a piece of paper and pen.

I have found that sometimes it is hard to dream and visualize what is possible for you. So… I want to give you permission to dream… and think about, and then journal it. Why? Because the writing causes the thinking.

What would your life look like if…

- You earned 10x more income
- Your relationships with family and friends were 10x better
- You attracted 10x more clients for your services
- You could purchase the house of your dreams now
- You could purchase the car(s) of your dreams now
- You could travel 10x more and to exotic places
- Other?

This may seem a little uncomfortable. It may seem a little farfetched. But that is exactly the point. You need to move yourself off the logical hamster wheel and begin to fantasize about what you really and truly want in your life.

Now lean into those dreams by employing H.A.R.D. Goals

In the book *H.A.R.D. Goals* by Mark Murphy (2010), he outlines a very useful concept which I have found to help people create goals for more effective change.

H.A.R.D. goals are:

- *Heartfelt* — My goals will enrich the lives of somebody besides me — customers, the community, etc.
- *Animated* — I can vividly picture how great it will feel when I achieve my goals.
- *Required* — My goals are absolutely necessary to help this company.
- *Difficult* — I will have to learn new skills and leave my comfort zone to achieve my assigned goals for this year.

H for Heartfelt:

No matter how evolved we think we are, we are ruled by our emotions. It has been said that the more emotionally attached we are to our goals, the greater the likelihood is that we will achieve them.

- Do you have an emotional attachment to your goal?
- Does it move you toward a desired future or help you prevent an undesirable one?

What we want to do is really feel our goals through our heart because this will increase the motivational power you put behind making your goals happen.

A for Animated:

This is all about visualizing your goal.

Close your eyes for a moment and picture how your life will be different once you have achieved your goal. What you want to do is create a vivid moving picture or a movie of your goals in your mind.

To do that, you will need to give it a perspective as to size, color, setting, background, lighting, emotions, and movement.

Then, you want to connect in a deep way. The more you are able to create this moving picture of your life as though the goal has been achieved, the more magnetic that future will become for you... and the more you'll want to work toward the goal.

I am sure you won't be surprised to learn that *"vision" is the driver behind achieving your goals.* Your brain can't tell the difference between reality and imagination. The more you replay your "movie" of your vision, the closer you will get to achieving your goal.

R for Required:

The more urgency you have around what you're working toward, the more likely you are to reach it. Maybe *obsessive* is too strong a word – but then again, maybe not.

Think about this: Is your goal absolutely necessary for your own or your company's success?

For example, if you run an eCommerce website and online sales are low, a goal to increase online sales would be a high requirement.

Also required: Give procrastination (which kills far too many goals) the boot. When you convince yourself and others of the absolute necessity of your goals, you make the future payoffs of your goal appear far more important and satisfying than what you can get today.

- What do you need to have accomplished by 6 months to keep on track toward achieving this goal?
- What about by the end of the next 90 days?
- The next 30 days?
- What's one thing you can accomplish today to pull you closer to your goals and dreams?

D for Difficult:

We all love a challenge, don't we? Goals that require us to learn new skills and expand ourselves are an inspiration.

To succeed with this, the goal needs to be sufficiently difficult to move us from our comfort zone.

- What are the 3-5 most important skills you'll need to develop to achieve this goal?
- How will you develop those skills?

I believe H.A.R.D. Goals will help push and challenge you to achieve great things, but that still isn't the whole story (gotta have a tweak).

You don't know what you don't know... like turning your annual income into your monthly income (What?)

I remember hearing this and was so skeptical... My conscious mind said, "You can't do that! This is just pure crazy-pants talk." But a part of me was intrigued... what if this were true? And if it was, I wanted to learn how to do it.

What if I could take my dream – my vision – and turn it into a goal? If I could really achieve that goal, how would that improve me (the bottom-line results of my life)?

What I have learned is that the true purpose of our goals is to help us grow. We have a basic human need to experience increase, not disintegration.

I also learned that when I wasn't aligned with my goals, I wasn't using my creativity in solving how to get from A to B... but rather "brute force." This always happened when the goal was set by someone else, or what I thought someone else wanted from me.

Goal achievement is a highly creative process

Later in my career, when I became the "owner" of my goals, I found I was much more energized and engaged in doing the work. That, in turn, boosted my creativity in figuring out how to achieve my goals.

In order for your mind to be truly engaged in the process, you need to go after a goal that you don't know how to do. When you set Big Goals, you are not meant to know how to get there... yet. This is where you need to allow yourself to get into a creating state.

You already have potential within you to reach these big beautiful goals. *Just Do It!*

You know deep down that you are capable of doing better. In fact, you haven't even scratched the surface as to what you are capable of. Lean into those dreams that seem like a fantasy.

Accept them, work toward them, believe in them!

The point is to dream big dreams and to be connected with something that *sets your heart on fire – that passion within you!*

I learned long ago, all of us were meant to thrive. And we were not put on this planet to just struggle or question or wonder or worry. We have been put on this planet to really live a beautiful life, to serve others and to bring out the best in you and those around you.

Ready to create the life you want?

Ready to create goals and dreams worthy of you?

Your next logical step is to get your goals and dreams "out of your head" and "on to paper."

To get your process started, I invite you to visit

www.coachbarbaraharrington.com/h-a-r-d-goals

and claim your free H.A.R.D. Goals Worksheet

Then, let's talk about what you really would like to change and improve about your results in your business and your life, because you *can*, even if you have tried and failed in the past.

BARBARA HARRINGTON

BARBARA HARRINGTON is an award-winning chemist (30+ years with a master's degree; featured on ABC, NBC, Fox News; Forbes Coaches Council Member) turned certified professional coach.

She have been coaching since the '90s... but was formally certified in 2015 as a certified professional coach from ICCA (International Coach Certification Alliance); Financial Coach in 2013.

As a respected chemist and scientist in her field, she recognized that people interact with others in much the same predictable way that chemical reactions do.

She is obsessed with how the brain works and solves problems. As a chemist, she naturally saw the connections between seemingly unrelated things to help her figure out the root cause of problems.

Everything Barbara does revolves around her passion for successfully helping others transform their lives.

She helps people make needed changes to transform their lives providing information, guidance, and support through Smart, Thoughtful, Excellent, and Mindful Coaching (S-T-E-M).

As your Business Coach, Barbara will help you identify the issues that are holding you back, and provide simple step-by-step framework that is scientifically (brain-based) proven to get you back on track to achieving *all* of your goals.

If you would like to get in touch with Barbara, email her at:

Barbara@CoachBarbaraHarrington.com

www.CoachBarbaraHarrington.com

TOO BUSY TAKING CARE OF BUSINESS...

CATHY FROST

AS AN ENTREPRENEUR WORKING ALONE or with just a small group of people, it's easy to become so intent on taking care of our clients or customers that we forget (or don't take the time) to take care of ourselves.

You may have heard that "sitting is the new smoking!" However, new research shows it depends on the type of sitting. Those who work in large offices get up to go to meetings, the copy machine, the water cooler, etc. It's binge sitting – sitting more than four hours – that has the biggest negative effect on your health.

As entrepreneurs, we may not have the same opportunities to run down the hall to a meeting. The printer might be within arm's reach and the meeting is often on the web – no walking required. Instead we should think about getting up more frequently (every 45-60 minutes) to increase movement and activity.

More of us are finding our metabolism slowing and it is difficult to lose weight and keep it off.

Now here's the thing – you can *unlock your metabolism* just by *eating real foods and improving your hydration.* That is what I encourage you to focus on – eating real foods and increasing hydration so you can create lasting habits to not only supercharge your metabolism but keep it revved up for years to come!

There are so many products on the market today claiming to help you lose weight quickly, yet after following them and losing some pounds, the weight comes back almost as fast as you lost it!

Over the past 32 years, I have personally helped more than 5,000 people create lasting weight loss and improve their health. During this time I have come to understand why...

Diets Don't Work!

Through my Forget Diets Forever program, I empower and equip clients with new discoveries and techniques to create and establish skills and habits to regain control of their lives – boosting their metabolism, creating lasting weight loss, improving their health, happiness, and love for themselves and others.

Are you frustrated with the weight loss game? Do you know your health could be improved with simple food and lifestyle changes? Have you realized that you can't keep doing the same things and expecting different results?

Then read on!

It's NOT Your Fault

Before you can supercharge your metabolism, it's important to understand *why* it has slowed to *prevent* it from slowing again.

Yes, age can play a part, but it doesn't need to!

After age 40, most people lose ½-pound of muscle each year. At first this may not seem like much, but at 50 they have lost 5 pounds of muscle. Since a pound of muscle burns 35-50 calories/day, when you multiply that by 5 pounds lost, their metabolism has already slowed 175-250 calories each day.

However, this can even be worse because research shows 25-30% of weight lost while dieting is lean muscle. People think it is mainly fat and just a little water weight – but *wrong!*

For every 10 pounds lost while dieting, about 3 pounds is muscle, which means your metabolism just decreased by another 105-150 calories per day... 735-1,050 calories/week!

This may not seem significant, but over the course of a month, this adds up to 3,150-4,500 *fewer calories* that your body will need to continue the lifestyle you have been living. *Remember, a pound of fat is about 3,500 calories.* Unless you are increasing your daily activity to burn an extra 150 calories, you will begin to regain fat as your metabolism is now *slower* than before you began your diet.

It also means your resting metabolism is now even *lower* than before you started the diet in the first place – when you thought you had gained weight because of a *slow metabolism.*

Another problem with calorie restriction (dieting) is your body enters starvation mode, and *will preserve fat for energy while burning muscle.* Fat is the last thing to go before you die of starvation.

This is why about 95% of those who lose weight on a diet regain most, or even more than, what they lost. *It's NOT the dieter's fault, it's the diet's fault!*

You think, "If I only had more willpower" – but again, that's not true! What the diet program forgot to mention is that *dieting decreases your willpower!*

Your brain uses glucose to fuel the energy source of willpower

When engaging willpower by giving up certain foods or creating new habits, your brain requires a large supply of glucose. Glucose comes from carbohydrates such as grains, fruits, and sweets – which most diets restrict. If you do not have ample glucose, your willpower will decrease, making it harder to build new habits.

And so the vicious cycle begins. Dieting causes you to not have enough glucose to fuel your willpower, yet you need willpower to eat less! It's not that you don't have willpower, it's that your brain is not getting enough glucose to fuel all the willpower the diet requires.

You have been misled by the diet industry, but that all ends *today!*

YES – What you eat and drink does matter...

Over the past 32 years of my coaching, one of the big things I have found is many people don't eat enough!

Now I never encourage calorie counting, as your body doesn't handle all types of food calories the same. Some have a higher TEF than others. What does that mean? When you eat, some of the calories are used for digestion. This is called the thermic effect of food (TEF). Studies have shown that the body uses twice the energy to break down foods containing protein as it does carbohydrates or fat.[1]

Adding protein has been shown to boost metabolism and increase the amount of calories burned by about *80 to 100 per day*.[2] Plus increasing your protein will help you feel full faster so you eat less calories throughout your day, gradually losing weight.

I know from the thousands of clients I have worked with that this is often the *best* and easiest thing you can do! We all need protein to ensure our muscles and the rest of our body are properly nourished, however, many people do not eat enough.

So how do you do it? Make sure you are adding more protein every time you eat. Even include protein in your snacks. Selecting good proteins in right amounts can *supercharge* your metabolism and provide the quick energy and metabolism boost you are desiring.

It really can be easy and you will love the results. By the way, protein is effective in minimizing belly fat!

The other good news is that once you have lost weight in this manner, continuing to eat a proper balance of protein will help keep the weight off.

Good sources of protein are skinless chicken and turkey, fish especially the fatty fish such as salmon, sardines, albacore tuna, and lake trout, plus other fish like cod, herring, perch rainbow trout, striped bass and shrimp, lean cuts of pork and beef, eggs, quinoa, lentils, nuts like almonds and peanuts, Greek yogurt, cottage cheese and milk.

Protein is a must to boost your metabolism.

---

[1] https://www.healthline.com/nutrition/how-protein-can-help-you-lose-weight#section2
[2] https://www.ncbi.nlm.nih.gov/pubmed/11838888

Foods to give your metabolism an extra boost

Green Tea – many studies show it is great for boosting metabolism. A cup of green tea in the afternoon could also help protect your body from disease-causing radicals, which have been linked to prostate and breast cancers due to its rich antioxidant content!

Spices like cayenne, black pepper, ground ginger, and chili powder all increase metabolism. The affects are greatest for those unaccustomed to eating spicy foods. Go ahead and spice up your meals to improve your metabolism.

Hot peppers can also heat up your metabolism. The capsaicin (chemical compound in spicy peppers) give them their heat and keeps your calorie-burning elevated long after you finish the meal.

Nuts and seeds are great, especially almonds which are nutritionally dense. Packed with macronutrients plus plenty of protein, fiber, and heart healthy monounsaturated fat, walnuts are a great source of omega-3 fatty acids and can also boost your cognitive function.

Chia seeds contain omega-3 and a great balance of soluble and insoluble fiber that keep your blood-sugar steady and boost your metabolism. They are great added to yogurt or on a salad.

Blueberries are packed full of antioxidants, which improves metabolism significantly. Plus they are a great source of fiber and help reduce inflammation.

Avocados have about 4 grams of protein and all 9 amino acids our body needs, including omega-3. Avocado greatly improves metabolism and is good for weight loss. For those who don't enjoy fatty fish, try using avocado more often. It can also help reduce stress and improve your skin.

Broccoli helps you burn calories faster because it is rich in both calcium and vitamin C. The calcium activates your metabolism and the vitamin C helps absorb the calcium – a win, win.

Spinach provides a nice dose of iron that carries oxygen to our muscles. Oxygen is needed in the muscles to burn fat. Our muscles will be able to burn fat at a faster rate with plenty of iron. Spinach helps protect against osteoporosis, heart disease, colon cancer, arthritis, and other diseases.

Greek yogurt is another excellent source of calcium and protein.

Celery is packed with fiber, water, and is low in calories. Because celery requires a lot of energy to digest, it shifts metabolism into a higher gear.

Whole eggs are packed with vitamin D. Our muscles need plenty of vitamin D to help build and repair them and it is essential in boosting metabolism.

Water is essential. Mild dehydration slows metabolism – so being well hydrated will keep your metabolism running higher.

Water ... make it COLD

It's important to start drinking more water – and it's even better if you make it COLD! Cold water must be warmed by your body, increasing your metabolism instantly. But when you're not properly hydrated, your metabolism slows even more dramatically.

Studies show you can increase your metabolism by 30% as well as aid weight loss – just by drinking 2 cups of water before a meal.[3] We can misinterpret thirst with hunger and mistakenly eat more than needed.

How much should you drink each day? The optimal amount depends on your weight, but I recommend you start out by drinking *at least 64 ounces* each day.

To more closely determine your ideal water intake, complete this formula:

_____ (pounds you weigh) ÷ 2 = _____ ounces you should drink for more optimal hydration.

Other benefits of drinking water include improved mental focus, skin tone, and relief of headaches.

---

[3] https://academic.oup.com/jcem/article/88/12/6015/2661518

For those who don't like plain water, you could...

Flavor your water – but only with natural things like a slice of lemon, lime, cucumber, or fruit such as strawberries, raspberries, blueberries, mango, etc.

Purchase bottled waters with natural flavors, but avoid water that is sweetened or has artificial sweeteners added. Artificial sweeteners have been shown to cause insulin resistance which can lead to diabetes. Artificially sweetened fluids are *not* a healthy alternative.

This same thing is true with diet sodas – they actually encourage fat storage! If you must drink a diet beverage, make sure you are doing it with a meal or snack that contains both protein and carbohydrates. When combined with other foods, the carbohydrates will contain real sugar which digests to glucose and requires insulin.

What about sparkling mineral water, club soda or seltzer – what is the difference? They are all types of carbonated water. They are all suitable alternatives in keeping you hydrated, and offer an *excellent change in flavor*.

Plus it has been found that drinking sparkling water has added health and weight loss benefits. It adds variety to help reach your hydration goals, plus it can also help improve digestive symptoms, constipation and gallbladder emptying!

So if you are finding it difficult or boring to always drink enough plain water – try adding some sparkling water!

Caution: Sweetened carbonated beverages have been linked to weight gain, obesity, kidney disease, insulin resistance, and an increased risk of heart disease, cancer, gout, and dementia!

Also, don't swap these bubbly waters for Tonic water, which is high in calories and sugar!

Your best water schedule:

- ☐ Upon rising – 8 oz. of warm water with juice from ½ lemon – a natural detoxifier which helps aid the liver in proper metabolism

- ☐ Coffee at least 30 minutes after the lemon water. The caffeine will help get your metabolism going, but caffeine has a diuretic effect, so I usually recommend not counting coffee in your daily water intake.

- ☐ 9:00 AM – 8 oz. ice water

- ☐ 11:30 AM – (or 30 minutes before you plan to eat lunch) 8 oz. ice water

- ☐ 12:00 PM - 8 oz. with your lunch – sparkling water is a great choice especially if you are accustomed to having soda with lunch. You are now halfway to your 64 oz. goal!

- ☐ 2:00 PM – 8 oz. cold water – will also greatly help hydrate your brain and afternoon focus and alertness

- ☐ 3:30 PM - 8 oz. Green tea – either warm or cold – preferably unsweetened. Besides its many health benefits, green tea is a great aid for weight loss. Again, the caffeine will boost your metabolism. I would not recommend counting green tea toward your hydration goal as it has more of a diuretic effect.

- ☐ 5:30 PM – (or 30 minutes before your evening meal) 8 oz. cold water or sparkling water

- ☐ 6:00 PM – 8 oz. cold or sparkling water with your meal

- ☐ 8:00 PM – relax with an 8 oz. cup of caffeine-free tea – I prefer one with chamomile which has a calming effect and may induce sleep. Caffeine-free teas do count toward your hydration goal and you have just achieved 64 oz. of hydration today!

Keeping track as you go is the best way to ensure exactly how much you are drinking. So copy this form as an easy way to track your progress.

Just a side note – I often find people trying to grab a very large water bottle so they will be more likely to drink more. However, I suggest using a container between 8–12 ounces. That way you will need to get up and refill it more often – a hidden way to sneak in a few extra steps and also move your body!

Breakfast – Non-Negotiable!

Skipping breakfast will instantly slow your metabolism. While you were sleeping, your body was conserving calories, so eating a balanced breakfast stimulates your metabolism as you start your day.

I'm sure you would never get in your car and expect it to function with no gas in your tank. The car must be fed with gas (or maybe electricity) to work. So we really should feed our body first thing in the morning to help it run its best.

Breakfast should also be eaten within 60 minutes after rising. If you wait and eat breakfast at work, that is probably too late – it's more likely a snack.

To supercharge your metabolism and keep it high, you *must* have some protein at breakfast. A quick bagel or muffin with your coffee is *not* a metabolism booster.

Lunch – Not Worth Skipping

In my practice, I have seen too many people who either don't take time for lunch or under-eat. A small yogurt or plain small salad without protein is not a metabolism-boosting lunch.

Skipping lunch also causes a bigger afternoon slump, which makes you twice as likely to grab something less than healthy – either sweet or salty – later in the afternoon.

Your brain needs lunch. When you skip lunch, your blood sugar decreases, which can decrease your ability to think clearly. Your brain needs glucose to run efficiently and if it doesn't have enough, it will not function as effectively. To be at your best, you must fuel your brain properly.

Lunch should have plenty of protein, a good size serving of vegetables, and a smaller serving of carbohydrates.

Dinner can be EASY

After a long hard day, it might seem difficult to prepare a well-balanced meal. But eating dinner is very important not only in supercharging your metabolism, but in keeping it high. Planning a little in advance can make dinner easy.

Like lunch, protein is a must for dinner. The easiest prep is just to roast some veggies and grill or bake a protein source. Check the end of this article for a link to obtain specific recipes.

Sleep

Lack of sleep can decrease the number of calories you burn and lower your metabolism plus it messes with how your body processes carbohydrates and can encourage you to eat more junk foods and sweets!

How much sleep should you strive for? It really depends on the individual, but 7-9 hours per night is recommended. Today, about 40% of our population is sleep deprived. If you are included in this statistic I encourage you to try to increase your sleep.

If you feel you have too much to do to get 7-9 hours of sleep – think again. With the proper amount of sleep, your productivity, energy, efficiency, and overall health will improve! You'll get more done and feel better while doing it.

Taking Care of Business

As entrepreneurs, it's important that we not only focus on our growing business, but also on taking care of ourselves, because you are the most important asset in your business! Without you, where would your business be?

Investing in yourself – to keep your body running at its peak – is just as important as investing in the best coach or the newest tech!

We only have one body, so nourishing and caring for it well should be just as important as taking care of your biggest customers. It really doesn't need to be complicated! Just ensure you are eating three balanced meals which include good protein, staying well hydrated, moving more, and getting enough sleep. These four simple things can greatly help your business as you will have more physical, mental, and emotional energy to best serve your clients and customers!

To help you create lasting weight loss, I invite you to visit 4easystepstoskinnyjeans.com to claim your free copy of *4 Easy, Simple Steps to Fit Into Your Skinny Jeans.* To learn more, plus get meal-planning strategies and easy, tasty healthy recipes for breakfast, lunch, snacks and dinner.

CATHY FROST

CATHY FROST is a Certified Integrative Wellness and Life Coach who has been an expert and leader in the Health and Wellness Field for more than 30 years. She is the founder of Forget Diets Forever and has personally helped more than 5,000 women create lasting weight loss and improve their health.

During this time she has come to understand why... Diets Don't Work & It's *Not* the Dieter's Fault! It's the *Diet's Fault!*

Through Cathy's Forget Diets Forever programs, she empowers and equips you with unique techniques to create skills and habits for designing your personal success path that boosts your energy and metabolism, creates lasting weight loss, improves overall health happiness, and love for yourselves and others, without giving up the foods you love.

She has served as a hospital Wellness Coordinator, Life Style Coach and Nutritionist with a large medical center and was the owner of five women-only fitness centers.

Learn more at www.forgetdietsforever.com.

STANDING ON THE SHOULDERS OF GIANTS

CHERYL SCHINDLER

There was no welcome party — no rule books.

Just wicked problems to overcome!

ROBERT FROST WROTE: "Two roads diverged in a wood, and I took the one less traveled by, and that has made all the difference." When facing challenges, I've created profound results by bulldozing a different path, away from the noise and people sleepwalking through life going nowhere fast.

I grew up as far as you can get from Silicon Valley, Wall Street, or the ivory towers that grace Ivy League schools. When people ask me where I'm from, I answer, "You go to nowhere, hang a right, and go eight more miles." My grandparents raised me on their farm near the Savannah River plant on the South Carolina/Georgia line. They instilled wisdom, values, and perseverance. I rose from a difficult background with humble beginnings and the odds stacked against me. That's how I know; if I can do it, you can too.

People often ask what my "secret" is to connecting with people. They want to know how I'm able to make such a powerful impact, gain support, and achieve remarkable outcomes.

If you've ever worked with me or attended one of my workshops or trainings, you'll know much of my success lies in knowing how – and where – to use Strategic Intelligence to create innovative solutions to open doors, build trust, solve problems, and quickly overcome challenges. These creative solutions increase positive outcomes, typically in a much shorter period of time. They are game changers – saving time, money, energy, and lead to higher ROIs.

Well, here's one of my secrets: I use "organic" and Social Media Information to develop Strategic Intelligence and use it to create solutions.

To clarify, "organic" information is information gathered outside of the internet. Social Media Information is information found on social media sites like Facebook, LinkedIn, Instagram, Twitter, Pinterest, and the plethora of other online sites.

When Social Media Information is collected, processed, analyzed and used, it becomes Strategic Intelligence. Strategic Intelligence provides a foundation for quickly building solid relationships, earning trust and respect, providing a higher level of service, and strategically positioning services and products to help clients. It allows you to dramatically separate yourself from the competition by showing that you value your clients, and their time, and it sets you up to become a trusted advisor.

Today, Social Media Information is easily accessible and one of the most valuable resources. Unfortunately, many people do not understand how or where to use this information or how to turn it into Strategic Intelligence to streamline the accomplishment of their goals and objectives, and to increase profits. This is one of my greatest talents and has provided the key to accomplishing things beyond my wildest imagination. If you're not on this path, the time for you to start is now!

Where Courage Comes From...

Problems Are Opportunities

Everyone already knows, solving challenging situations requires laser focus. Too often, when failing, what people don't have is a willingness to adjust their strategy as things unfold. The road to success in business, and especially in marketing and sales, is not always a straight line.

You've Come a Long Way, Baby

There was no welcome party — no rule books. Just wicked problems to overcome!

The exhilaration of my being promoted to a highly respected pharmaceutical company, Lederle Labratories' prestigious Hospital Representative position at Duke University Medical Center, shattered the day I arrived. Within hours, I realized the current state of affairs were far worse than I'd been told. My mission was to rebuild Lederle's account at Duke, redeem Lederle's reputation, create long-term positive relationships after 17 years of missteps, and dramatically increase sales. I wasn't sure which was needed more — miracles or an entire team of guardian angels.

Grasping the reality of the situation, it became clear to me there was only one way to go, and that was up! I intended to use it to my advantage.

A little necessary background first...

Doctors in teaching hospitals are extremely busy, focusing on patients, consulting, teaching residents, working with fellows, participating in research, publishing articles, and the likes. Extremely fortunate reps may get lucky and be granted one brief appointment with a prestigious doctor. The rep's hope of getting a second appointment is contingent on her ability to provide value and genuine services... something those before me had taken for granted. I'm not a pharmacist or a doctor and I didn't play one on TV. Most of what I had going for me was sheer determination, grit, and a tenacious spirit to find innovative and creative solutions to see the docs and earn their trust.

A New Direction

I persuaded the Pro at the sports club down the street from Duke University Medical Center to sell me inexpensive passes to distribute to some of my doctors. As I explained, this was a win-win-win opportunity. I'd give the passes to the doctors of my choice. The doctors would have a chance to experience the club, and that would provide a simple path for the sports club to increase their memberships. It was a sweet deal for the club as I was basically underwriting and running their membership campaign!

The racquetball Pro (my new Giant in Training) had his office down a narrow hallway across from the racquetball courts. Okay, I may have mentioned the names of doctors who were most important to me. Imagine the coincidence. I just happened to know when my target doctors had reservations to play racquetball. My being in that narrow hallway leading to the racquetball courts, talking to the Pro or other club members when my target doctors were arriving or departing – that was no accident!

I accomplished far more in those brief encounters with docs at the sports club than I could have during the usual hustle and bustle at the medical center in months. The relationships built at the health club flourished, and as a result, so did everything else I was sent to Duke to accomplish.

Money cannot buy the education I got from spending three years at Duke University Medical Center among the best of the best healthcare providers while learning to maneuver amidst power, politics, ego, and money. It was at Duke that many of my successful processes were created, tested, and refined. Because they can be life changing, many of these lessons are covered in my training programs.

Standing on the Shoulders of One Special Giant

Carl Merideth, Pharm. D, M.B.A., was the Hospital District Manager to whom I reported. God had placed the perfect man in my path to become my mentor and to support me through this quagmire. Carl recognized my tenacious spirit and unique ability to orchestrate positive outcomes quickly and efficiently. He embraced my critical thinking and gave me free rein to try approaches no one else had even considered. It's amazing how empowering it can be to have someone behind you who believes in you!

Hiding in Plain Sight

Critical Thinking + organic/Social Media Information + Strategic Intelligence = Greater Success

This universal formula is extremely powerful, producing results faster with higher profitability. If you follow this process it will help you understand and align with your customers, and that leads to greater success. Time and time again, very dependably, this formula has proven beneficial for my clients, former employers, family, and me for decades. And it'll work for you.

My Life's Playbook

My God-given gift is an innate talent to circumnavigate what most believe is obvious in a problem and see solutions with crystal clarity. To discover innovative solutions, you first have to see past what everyone else believes is obvious. This is a skill you can learn.

Under a great deal of stress, I was once in the process of searching for specific information on federal and state mediation laws. I wasted $1,000 meeting with three credentialed attorneys that led to no ROI. None.

Out of time, low on funds and fighting a sinking feeling of desperation, I changed tactics. I decided to research the top law school in our state to find someone who actually taught federal and state mediation law. In less than 10 minutes, I found two law school professors whose CVs were sterling. After briefly studying my online findings and the law professors' photos, I decided to contact one using an empowering email. I had nothing to lose. This professor graciously provided the much-needed answers and issued his opinion on the document... all at no charge.

I believe everything we need in life is available to us.
We just have to have courage,
learn how to make critical connections,
call in what's needed, believe and take action.

Value of Using Social Media Information
and Strategic Intelligence

As you can see, sales and product training may not be enough. Innovative critical thinking, Social Media Information, and Strategic Intelligence were required to expedite solutions. I've spent my entire life using these formulas to swiftly solve problems and position myself for the highest levels of success. It's an innate talent honed by sheer necessity.

As of July 2019, there were over 4.3 billion active internet users, and 3.5 million of those were active on social media sites. For you to achieve the success you are seeking, it's crucial for you to understand how to use social media information to open doors, help you better serve your clients, and increase your ROI, whether you're an individual, small business, or a Fortune 100 or 500 company. Please pause and think about how this can greatly benefit you.

"Only 24% of buyers found that salespeople

are knowledgeable about their specific business."

— Forrester Research

This is not theory or smoke and mirrors...

Genuinely Care... Authenticity

A few years ago, I was charged with selling a painting to a past president of a global textile company. During an annual meeting, there were about 50 textile men — many legends — socializing at a resort. Striking up a conversation with the past president, I congratulated him on one of his successes in working with his local organization and their receiving the distinguished safety award. He stopped in his tracks and his jaw dropped. Looking around the room, he pointed to the attendees and said, "I've known most of these men for 40 or 50 years. Some longer. None of them know about my work with that hospital or the award. Thank you."

You guessed it... the painting sold in that brief encounter for 100% of the asking price.

In our fast-paced world filled with noise and diminishing human interactions, many people hunger for caring connections and authentic relationships. The example above is one of hundreds that show the value of strategically using Social Media Information and Strategic Intelligence to gain respect, build valuable relationships, and set yourself apart from the masses. It's a way of showing people you really do care – and it builds successful outcomes.

Overcoming Complicated Problems with Simple Solutions

Bob Fritzky, President of MET (Medical, Economic and Technological) Solutions, recruited me to be the Senior Director, Pharmaceutical Initiatives when he started the consulting company. Our clients were Big Pharma powerhouses including Merck, Glaxo Welcome, Pfizer, Roche, Novartis, and Eli Lily. MET Solutions was a division of Bozell, Jacobs, Kenyon and Eckhardt – the "Got Milk" advertising campaign. Our silver bullet was our stellar team, and the use of Strategic Intelligence. We created cutting-edge solutions unimpeded by traditional means.

This is my wheelhouse and why I was assigned to this situation.

One of our big pharma clients had a complicated problem developing fair budgets for their smoking cessation drug. I met with the National Sales Manager and his team. We discussed the challenges and how MET Solutions' Strategic Intelligence initiatives could provide a custom comprehensive solution that would save the company millions of dollars. After reviewing the clear and simple solution I provided, the client immediately signed our $500,000 agreement.

R-E-S-P-E-C-T (Thanks, Aretha Franklin)

Another CEO was looking forward to the session he'd booked with us to reward his top three sales representatives. The reps arrived early. The CEO, who was a stickler for being on time, was late. As the minutes passed, everyone grew more concerned. To make matters worse the CEO did not answer his cell. A half hour passed.

That's when we heard the front door of the club open. There was urgency in the fast approaching footsteps.

Stressed, our missing guest had arrived. We got him seated and offered a cup of coffee. As he calmed down, one of his reps asked, "What happened?" The CEO paused, settled himself and said, "On my way here I got a speeding ticket." Everyone was respectfully silent. Then one rep said respectfully, "It's too bad the officer didn't give you a warning."

In a somber tone – and with a smile – the CEO looked up and replied, "The trooper was very nice. He said he'd considered doing that but he couldn't... because I passed the car he was chasing!"

It's Your Insurance Policy

These simple, universal principles are powerful and effective and can be applied in your life and your business, uncomplicating the most challenging situations. The process I am offering you is for anyone who wants a better life or is facing challenging situations – regardless of who you are, where you live, which industry you're in, or what type of clients you work with. It provides the intelligence to open doors, make connections with the right people, and helps you help those you serve by delivering a much greater level of success... often making the seemingly impossible possible.

Simply put, this process is for you. Every problem has a solution. Goals are achievable.

- I've developed these strategies into a proven system that *anyone* can use to get consistent, repeatable results.
- It doesn't matter what industry or profession you work in – this training will show *you* how to be more successful and help you reach your full potential.
- You'll emerge from this training with a broader understanding, enlightened and utterly transformed.
- Just imagine the life-changing process *you* will go through as you immerse yourself in learning, living and breathing these concepts.

These simple, universal principles are powerful and effective and can be applied in your life and your business, uncomplicating the most challenging situations. I say this with conviction and without any reservations because these principles do work. They can make your life easier and help you achieve more. That's not an opinion or speculation but a time-proven truth.

CHERYL SCHINDLER

CHERYL SCHINDLER is the President of AMillion Inc., a strategic solutions company specializing in the use of social media intelligence to help clients find innovative solutions to challenging problems. Street wise with extensive business knowledge, Cheryl holds decades of corporate and small business experience in management, sales, marketing, and advertising to significantly increase ROI. Along with her long list of notable achievements in the business world, Cheryl's most valued and respected talent is teaching *unique, proven ways* to connect with clients – overcoming seemingly impossible challenges – to orchestrate the desired, positive outcomes.

www.amillioninc.com
cheryl@amillioninc.com

When Success is Not Optional

The Truth... The Whole Truth...
and Nothing but the Truth

Daniel L. Schindler

BROKEN – HE DROVE FROM ONTARIO TO NORTH CAROLINA to work with me. Struggling in vain with a crippling disease, compounded by a long series of failures, this man clung to his weakening determination. All you had to do was look. It wasn't just the painful physical limitations, it was in his eyes. Hers too, desperately wanting to see her husband smile in earnest again. Because he loved this sport and refused to give up.

That was my assignment, a responsibility I take seriously with every student. At first, I misjudged just how deep his emotional despair really was. But only temporarily because when reality surfaced I *was* paying attention.

To lead efficiently and effectively, grit and determination won't compensate for a lack of competency. If you put your leadership on display without direction, that's a guaranteed formula for a mediocre performance. And, as an entrepreneur, you don't have time for mediocrity.

For decades I've been a full-time shotgun shooting instructor and coach. The clay target sports can be a serious endeavor, from weekend warriors to those who compete in the Olympic events. Teaching nationally and internationally, I've worked with thousands of students for nigh on four decades. My books are sold around the world. Hundreds of souls from all walks of life have rolled up their sleeves, trusted me and worked their way through my harder-than-rock Instructor certification classes. As a former Team USA All American; a certified N.S.C.A. Level III, U.S., I was the first American to be certified by the British Guild, U.K.

Thankfully, I had the experience and was prepared to help this Canadian. Because it sure wasn't all about his shooting.

The shooting skills he had, on the surface, were only his tools – just like your tools – the specialized talents you bring to your business. But what you may not realize is that some of your best prospects, clients, and customers will need more from you than just a good product or service. Sometimes, to excel in daily work, we are called to not only share our skills with the world, but to help repair the spirit of those we serve.

As the Canadian's lesson began, I noticed more than his physical restrictions. From my position behind him, his past failures were visibly hamstringing his efforts. And all the cheerleader talk in the world wasn't going to help. Every target miss was another crushing burden, pulling him helplessly down into that place he hated. Again.

His climb – our climb – out of that very dark hole was unkind. Neither of us had any room to spare. Every second counted. We needed success and right now. For that very reason, I had prepared for this day. And you can, too.

The stakes were high – for both of us. We were going up this hill *together*. What you may not realize yet, is that once your clients trust you, now they are really listening to you. You have their full attention. My client trusted, and neither of us fell. Hope was mounting. Hope that he actually could. Not mastering just the skill itself, but realizing that *he could do this!*

A long-absent confidence crept back into him, his victories finally dissipating into peaceful gratification. Done with what he'd come for, he asked me to sit under the pavilion with him and his wife. Head down, he put his face in his hands, immersing himself in the long awaited realization that *he actually could succeed!* His beaming wife and I remained quiet while he relished his right-here, right-now triumphs. This was a man who always knew he could do it... and now he was right.

Please tell me you understand, this was not all about his shooting.

When he shook my hand firmly, he now understood that he hadn't come for a shooting lesson. It was personal. And my message to you is this: *it was no more personal for him than me.*

Of course, the credit all goes to him. This man signed up. He showed up courageously and put in his time. He overcame the hardships. We need to recognize the circumstances that bring clients to our doorsteps, and why we must be prepared to exceed our customers' expectations – on time – dependably and competently.

This requires a process – a "system" held together by more than just *competence.* I'm talking about a non-negotiable competence – an art where your skills deliver a lot more than what your customer expected. Where does that skill – that level of competence – come from?

Here's the thing about learning. The learning doesn't come first. Accepting, yielding to another perspective has to come first. Learning follows. Maybe. Sometimes. It depends on how much we are open to paying attention during the lesson.

Millions have fallen short of their own expectations and their employer's expectations. As entrepreneurs, does this mean you as well? Too many choose to remain in their comfort zone, day after day with no motivation to change. When there's no work invested, no risks taken, no critical thinking – there's no lesson, no learning, no real advancement.

If, however, you are of a mind to be observant, I can provide you with a blueprint for success in business and life. I'm not offering you the magic beans for instant success, because the instant part is a seductive myth. I'm just saying I'm an older dog who knows how to get someone to share the couch and part with that last bite of steak.

Because you're reading this book, it suggests you might be at a crossroad. Have you thought long and hard about what you *really* want – where you want to go – not just short-term but long-term? No? That's OK. Learning comes in chapters. If you're open to listening to another perspective.

*"It ain't what we don't know that gets us in trouble.
It's what we know for sure that just ain't so."*
–Mark Twain

Each experience you have has come straight out of life's box of chocolates. Some of it will be painful. They say that's where the wisdom usually comes from. I've got a hard-earned pile of it.

Sometimes that requires failing. Which I've done in the past. You will have to face crossroad after crossroad. I frequently took the wrong turn and ran straight into the consequences. In the beginning, I couldn't see the advantages of this frustrating reoccurrence. Truth is, I wore my mentors out. My trial and error path did, however, finally lead me to a revelation. Those failures were a blessing.

Coming again to those same crossroads, I learned which turns not to take. As you face challenges each day in your business and personal life, remember that you will come to these crossroads.

I've learned that the direct approach – using facts – expedites progress and circumnavigates confusion and misunderstandings. When your best clients come to you for expertise, you must be prepared. Professional people will quickly recognize – and appreciate – when your work ethic is held to the very highest standards. Your customers will be expecting that from you.

What you need is a system that you and your clients can count on. Dependably. Consistently.

Maybe you're thinking our professions and our customers are not the same, so what's my point? My point is, they are the same – *success principles are universal.*

A few of my clients include Michelin, Milliken & Co., Dupont, Duke Power, Cummings, Pepsi, a United States Ambassador, Merrill Lynch, Bowater, Lockwood Green, a U.S. Nuclear Submarine group, doctors and lawyers, CEOs and CFOs of corporations, business owners, CPAs, engineers, and folks from all walks of life. I am grateful for their trust in me and their patronage.

What does it takes to measurably advance a skill, any skill?

> *"Perfection is achieved,*
> *not when there is nothing more to add,*
> *but when there is nothing left to take away."*
>
> *–Antoine de Saint-Exupery*

This is the secret. The Way. The very art of success with endless applications. Wanting to be profoundly good at something requires a major shift of your attention to that system. You must streamline that process until each successful next step becomes *instinctive."*

Successful people – truly successful people – have learned to focus on this formula, a system which substantially enhances outcomes. Unfortunately, that invaluable, immeasurably important discovery eludes many.

You probably have a small library of business books, audiobooks, and video courses on how to become more successful. But how much of that knowledge, that wisdom, and those systems have you actually put into place?

And what's stopping you?

After reading a million pages, listening to a billion spoken words, and relentless study, it seems too complicated. Only those who persevere extract the core principles. What is one next step you can enact *today* that will move you toward your larger goal?

The most successful entrepreneurs know how to make these principles flat out work. You can take that to the bank. They've developed an uncomplicated system that pares away the unnecessary and focuses unapologetically on achieving goals. And by using that system, *what profits their customers profits them.*

Our clients' challenge today is to separate those of us who really do know from those who claim to know and don't. Prudence suggests you be selective in whom you consult, whom you trust. We both understand that. The pretenders with a sharp appearance who dazzle with clichés too often create a false impression of competency. But they haven't put in the work, nor do they know how things *really* work. This will be underlined by their vague, practiced answers to unfamiliar questions. Showmanship gets substituted for true expertise.

So... how can you show up in the world with confidence and integrity, especially when your business brings you into unfamiliar territory? *Be the first to admit not knowing.* Consult with someone you trust. Then take your hard-earned lessons and apply them at the next crossroads, because success demands that you keep showing up.

My Canadian client was able to rise above his physical and emotional limitations because he trusted my simple methods. I'm recommending you begin to assemble strategies that consistently and inevitably work. Do not create conditions. And above all, do not create excuses. Just deliver a superior ROI.

A good Coach can change an outcome.
A great Coach can change a life.

Goals are wonderful but, as we know, future outcomes are unknown. However, what are known are your specific tasks – the non-negotiable success principles... the principles that ensure predictable, rewarding outcomes. If you or your group would like to engage in an insightful, meaningful session about these key principles, it would be my pleasure to work with you.

DANIEL SCHINDLER

DANIEL SCHINDLER, the Founder of Paragon School of Sporting Inc., is a Master Instructor who knows how to take challenging situations and create simple, easy-to follow systems and processes to achieve desired outcomes.

Dan is a published writer, an accomplished speaker, consultant, and inspiring teacher who has worked with thousands of students. His clients include US Ambassadors, C-Suite and Marketing Executives and people from all walks of life. Known nationally and internationally, Dan is one of the most respected shotgun Instructors in the world.

The skill development systems and processes he teaches have *universal* applications. They are not only business savvy but Life changing. Confirmed by client after client, Dan's recommendations – when implemented – appreciably improve relationships with personal and professional associates, clients, and potential customers as well. Predictably, these processes are more efficient and productive, thus fostering customer loyalty and improving ROI.

www.paragonschool.com
customerservice@paragonschool.com

THE REASON WORDS MATTER SO MUCH IN MARKETING

DENISE FAY

AT ANY POINT IN THE CLIENT JOURNEY, you will have customers in one of three phases:

- *Phase 1. Client Attraction.* It's the initial stage where someone notices you, or when you want them to notice you.
- *Phase 2. Client Conversion.* This is the phase where you'll spend most of your time, converting that initial attraction, nurturing the interest, and transforming it into buying.
- *Phase 3. Client Engagement.* This is the phase where you put a ring fence around the clients that you've just spent time and resources nurturing and turning them into a client.

This blueprint of ACE (Attract, Convert, and Engage) can be applied to any industry and any sector.

Marry me, Marry me... on a First Date?

The biggest phase of the customer journey is conversion. While many business owners focus on attraction, successful marketers spend their time and put effort into conversion. It is a wide-ranging phase – covering everything from written marketing material and sales techniques to closing strategies.

If you think about it, when you met your partner, you didn't ask that person to marry you straight away or expect to be asked... you got to know them, learned a bit more about them, and enjoyed the process. It's exactly the same with marketing.

Let me tell you that once you master the art of Conversion, your sales are going to go through the roof. Many of your competitors are screaming '*marry me today*' in their messaging. If nobody does that in the real world, then why do it in the business world? You will have the added advantage by asking your prospects to get to know you first.

One of the main, but often overlooked, ways in which you get to know people and gain a better understanding of them is through the words you use.

The Power of Conversion

I know only too well about the Power of Conversion. Phone call after phone call to my marketing agency, Achieve Marketing, said the same thing. *"We're sorry, Denise. It's not you, it's the recession."* The recession hit in late 2008 and my business had become a casualty. I went from working with numerous clients doing their outsource marketing to a client list that I could count on one hand. When I closed the doors for Christmas at the end of 2008, I wouldn't have dreamed any of that would happen in January 2009.

I had to do something. I turned to the one thing that I had a flair for... copywriting – in other words, using the written word to sell. I read everything I could, studied with the copywriting masters, and discovered the art and science of copy, the content that we use.

I wrote material that built relationships – emails, sales pages, blogs, social media content. Clients started seeing results. I had always been a good writer but through experimentation I discovered this hidden secret to successful marketing.

In school we are taught to write. However as business owners or executives, we aren't taught effective, converting ways to write. Yet our words are even more prevalent than they were several years ago.

Think about it:

- social media posts
- sales letters
- video sales letters
- videos scripts

- podcast scripts
- emails
- blogs
- content articles
- SEO articles
- social media ads
- Google ads
- Bing ads

...and the rest.

You see, the words you use on all written communication represent you 24/7/365 – so that's 24 hours a day, 7 days a week and 365 days a year. You yourself can only be in one place at one time but your words... well, they are everywhere.

They need to convert – both written and verbally.

Introducing Incongruence

Carl Rogers introduced the concept of incongruence to psychology in the 1950s. General use of the word has come to mean 'not the same, not compatible or out of place'.

It is an incredibly important concept in marketing. In essence, if something is wrong, your subconscious brain picks it up, not your conscious brain. Have you ever said to yourself that something isn't right, but yet you can't quite put your finger on it? Chances are, that's incongruence.

It happens all the time between meeting and talking to someone in-person versus reading something they've written. One could be very formal while the other is quite informal. Even though you aren't necessarily aware of it, expectations are set but when they aren't met, then there is a problem.

If it's online, your lead will bounce off right away. If it's in-person, they'll politely excuse themselves, never to come back.

Your words represent you – so they must be the same online as offline.

If you are going to convert a lead into a sale, and you use supporting marketing material to do that, then you need to get to grips with the wonders of the written word.

Here are five ways which you can use words to convert clients – time and time again.

1. Craft clever headlines

As we are in the converting phase, Phase 2, let's assume your reader or lead has found you attractive and wants to know more about you. How do you convert that attraction using the written word?

You start with your headline.

Radio WIIFM: There is a radio station that we are all tuned into – it's called Radio WIIFM.... *What's In It For Me?*

This has to be the biggest question to ask yourself because it's exactly what your reader is asking when they read anything you've written. Use your words to answer that question: "What's it in for me?" Then put yourself in your reader's shoes.

David Ogilvy, considered to be the Father of Advertising, had this to say about headlines:

> "On the average, 5 times as many read the headlines as read the body copy. It follows that unless your headline sells your product, you have wasted 90% of your money."

Headlines are not click bait, they are the gate-keepers to your copy. I believe that the purpose of the headline is to get people to read the next line. Your headline should sell you enough to get your prospect to read the next line and so forth until they get to the end.

What would you say if I told you that I could give you two solid gold techniques for writing headlines?

Would you say, "Yes please, Denise"?

On the balance of probability, you answered this question. As humans, we are programmed to answer. When we are asked a question, our brain's thought process is taken over, because questions trigger a mental reflex, and the question needs answering. Nothing else matters.

If I ask you the color of your eyes or where you grew up, instinctively you want to answer the question. This is a key emotion when it comes to converting clients and asking the right questions.

Therefore, questions make very powerful headlines. Here are some examples:

- What would an extra €5000 or $5000 mean to your business?
- Who else wants a celebrity figure?
- Want 31 ways to write better copy?

Once you know your audience, you should know what questions they would answer. If you are unsure or just starting out, it's time to test this technique.

Think about 'what's in it for me?' when you put your questions forward.

2. Create curiosity

Another great headline technique is to create curiosity. The scientists – neuroscience and psychology – have been studying curiosity for years. Curiosity is the seeking of knowledge.

Curiosity is considered an emotion and a huge motivator.

Look at the amount of time spent consuming information, chatting with friends, browsing the internet with no real purpose and all the windy roads it takes you, even rubber-necking at car accidents. It's our incessant need for knowledge. We are practically oblivious to its influence on our lives... until we stop and actually think about it (like today).

Just look at these curiosity-inducing headlines:

- The most expensive lesson you'll ever learn
- Advertising pays – but who gains?
- Want a Wonderful Warm Way to Welcome Winter?

- 5 Amazing Ways to Use Pasta You Never Knew Existed

These headlines compel us to want to know more. Use it to your advantage.

3. Use structure to entice

A lot of people struggle with structuring their writing. It's usually caused by bad habits picked up while at school or college.

Many business owners find it hard to break up text into paragraphs. A great rule of thumb is to start a new paragraph for every new idea. It just makes your copy flow better. It keeps you on point because you're only talking about one particular topic. Like this paragraph. We are only talking about a new idea, nothing else.

Another great rule of thumb is to think about the sentences within each paragraph. When it comes to structuring sentences, you don't want them to be too long. Otherwise, your readers will struggle to keep up with you. Use punctuation to create distinct phrases if you really feel like you can't write shorter sentences.

The test I use is a simple one I discovered a long time ago. Read the sentence aloud. If you're out of breath by the time you reach the full stop, you need to either shorten the sentence or break it into two separate sentences.

The worst offender I came across was a mammoth, 50-word sentence. That's a huge turn-off because your reader will struggle to understand the point you're attempting to make. Try it! You will be out of breath by the time you get to the end of a 50-word sentence. I'm a marathon runner, and I'd like to think I'm fit, but not after that 50-word sentence, I can tell you.

Here's my advice about structure – write the way you speak. Again another simple technique. Your copy should flow just as a conversation, so there will be times when you need to use long sentences (like this one). Other times, short is best.

If you take the time to structure your writing so it's easier for your reader to digest, they will return the favor by taking the time to read it.

The same goes for the words you choose. It's best to avoid jargon wherever possible. If you're writing about something a bit complicated, try using metaphors and similes to explain it.

You also want your writing to be clear and concise, so cut out any unnecessary words. Why use three words when one will do?

4. Reel them in with Magic

There is an art and science to written material. Writing is an art form. Just as artists have their oils and brushes, we writers have our own tools.

One of the tools is the clever use of literary devices. Literary devices include alliteration, hyperbole, metaphors, metonyms, oxymorons, and similes. These brilliant little techniques liven up copy and create magic. They help the reader to really understand, to use their imagination to see what you are selling... not just mere words on a page.

One of the curiosity-laden headlines listed above was '*Want a Wonderful Warm Way to Welcome Winter?*'

Not only does it take in curiosity, but it is also peppered with alliteration – where the same letter is used at the beginning of each word in a sentence.

It's so powerful. Even if it is a hundred degrees where you are, when reading this sentence you are transported to a place in your mind where you think about winter. *A warm, welcomed winter.*

For me, I'm thinking about drinking hot chocolate by a warm fire, with rain outside (in Ireland, we get more rain than snow!) and a great movie on the TV, snuggled up with my children.

That may not be your vision, but I can guarantee you thought about how you would welcome winter. See, that's the power of alliteration. It's individual to everyone, so you are appealing to everyone... just by a few simple word choices.

Other devices in addition to alliteration include 'hyperbole'. It's the use of exaggeration to emphasize a point. Statements such as "*I told you a million times," "I'm so tired I could sleep standing up,"* or *"These books weigh a ton,"* add drama into a sentence without being wildly dramatic.

Use devices like these and you'll see people read about your product or service with completely different eyes... and you will convert them. Your words fuel your prospect's imagination... and they become more than words – your prospect internalizes them and as a result you are elevated in their mind.

Compare your copy which fuels your prospect's imagination with boring old text on your competitor's social media or websites.

Imagine the difference? Good. Because that's what sets you apart from your competition. It helps nurture that relationship, which is exactly what we want.

5. Let it settle

An essential part of writing anything is to let it settle. This will help your conversion ratio – no matter the size of the content. Whether it is a blog, a video script, a social media post, or a 'straight to the point' sales email, the best thing to do is let it settle.

Good copy is like a pint of Guinness. In Ireland, this involves a time-honored ritual in two parts. First, the stout is filled three-quarters of the way and then it is let to settle for 119 seconds. Not the full two minutes, but 119 seconds. It is then topped up and presented to the customer.

It's the same with your copy. Take a break from writing. Go for a walk or do some other work, then come back to it 30 minutes later.

With fresh eyes, you'll spot spelling mistakes and other errors you hadn't seen before. You can't rely purely on a spellcheck.

The right words matter when you are trying to nurture a lead and convert them to a sale. If you take the time to write the right words, peppered with a little art and science of good copy techniques, then your sales conversion ratio will explode. The written word is more than just content, it's copy, it's emotion, it's your brand. It's your business written down. Take the time to build relationships with your prospects and you'll reap the rewards.

27 Ways to Write Headlines that Convert

Attraction is great but it's the converting that you need to work the most on. How do you convert? It's the words you use... whether on your marketing material or in your sales techniques.

You see, we are all tuned into our own radio – yes, you've got to break through the noise and get them to hear you. And how do you do that? With great use of headlines.

Then you move onto your body text and structure it carefully. Utilize underused techniques at your disposal that your competitors aren't. Take advantage of hyperbole and alliteration. Then let it settle before publishing.

As a gift, and as a way to get started, I'd like to give you "27 Headlines that Convert." They cover curiosity headlines, emotional headlines, command headlines, and news headlines. Two Advils will never resolve writer's block. Sometimes we all need a bit of extra help.

Download your free cheat sheet today.

www.27headlinesthatconvert.com

DENISE FAY

DENISE FAY is an award-winning author, TEDx speaker, podcaster, and international marketing communications mentor. Having had a successful corporate career with Fortune 500 multi-nationals, she set up her award-winning marketing agency in 2006. Achieve Marketing is a marketing communications agency that helps B2B small business owners who sell a service to stand out from a saturated market, win clients, and keep them for life.

She has recently been nominated as one of Ireland's most inspiring businesswomen.

If she's not doing marketing, then she's talking about it over at her new podcast, "Let's Talk Marketing with Denise Fay."

An avid runner, you'll often find her out running the roads of historic and scenic County Louth, Ireland, where she lives, or simply hanging out with her two children and husband.

www.denisefay.com

THREE KEYS TO DEEP CONNECTION WITH YOUR TRIBE

DIANA ASAAD

AS A COACH, CONSULTANT, OR EXPERT IN YOUR FIELD, you may have believed your prospects and clients were simply looking for a product or service you can provide, when in reality, more than half of what you do is counsel and advise people! Solving people's problems is not just a counseling skill, it is a life skill. When used effectively, this life skill can set you apart from your competition and create an audience of people who are waiting to hear from you.

I was recently at an event with Kim Walsh Phillips and I watched her dig deeper into the blocks that were holding back a participant. It seemed like every time Kim would suggest something to improve the participant's business, this lady had a reason why that would never work for her! After some carefully crafted questions, Kim seemed to hit the wall... but like the expert she is, she didn't let that stop her. Rather Kim plowed through it, getting right to the core issue at hand. This woman was feeling tremendous guilt for not being available to her family and feared that any higher level of success would take her away from them even further. She was self-sabotaging even before giving the suggestions a chance. Like a pro, I watched Kim carefully and caringly challenge her to move past and answer questions like, "What would it look like if you did succeed?" Slowly I watched this woman begin to believe in her own potential.

I couldn't let the moment pass before pulling Kim aside and letting her know that I thought she'd make a great counselor. Without missing a beat she replied, "I *counsel* people who won't go to get counseling." And immediately I drew the parallel. We are "counseling" people all the time. I aim to show you how to do it effectively and impactfully.

The relationships we build with our clients will often wind up including aspects of emotional or physical support, and are built on a foundation of mutual respect and trust. Not unlike other relationships in life, there can be a honeymoon phase when the client is enamored with the promise and newness of it all. But like anything in life worth having, the reality phase kicks in and they quickly realize that it may not be all gum-drops and roses. Business and relationships take work. And we often hit bumps along the way that hinder us or can make us throw in the towel altogether.

As an intensive crisis marriage counselor, I see couples struggling with cycles of defeat and hurt and wanting to give up as well. Using practical tools, I guide them to resolution on these very difficult relationship issues. Eighty-five percent of the couples that come see me in my practice are infidelity or broken trust cases, yet our success rate is over 93% of couples seeing better than expected results.

A common recurring pattern I see over and over in my practice is that we drift away from our loved ones when we feel we no longer matter to them. It is on a subconscious and fundamental level that this drift occurs, but it is nonetheless the thing that causes great divides in relationships. This same thing can occur between you and even your best clients, when over time they feel like they don't matter to you. Most of us get into these fields to help others as a primary goal, yet if we aren't careful, that focus can become auxiliary, and your clients (as well as your bottom line) will feel it!

As an expert, there is a way to use my principles of success for conflict resolution in any relationship. These methods are especially helpful for coach and client relationships. These simple techniques help you create a raving fan mentality in your tribe, all while serving your clients better.

Your potential clients want solutions, you have the solutions. What they need is to believe they can implement those solutions. We are not the only ones on earth with the answers, but what sets us apart is a connection to the audience that helps them see they don't have to be bound by their own limiting beliefs. Sell them what they want – the solution – and give them what they need – a way to see that they can be set free from limiting beliefs. All they have to do is get out of their own way.

Remember you may not be everyone's "flavor" and that's okay. Not everybody who likes Oprah likes Dr. Oz, and not everybody who likes Steve Harvey likes Oprah... there's a personality connection that also happens between client and provider. Know who you are called to and accept that not everyone likes the same "flavors." Embrace your special sauce and distinctive "flavor" and own your uniqueness and you will serve people richly.

But first, in order to accept influence from you, people must know you care and identify with something you offer on a deep level.

Key 1: They Matter

Coaching is about caring... seeing the potential in another person when they often don't see it for themselves. The secret key to serving others effectively is to make them feel like they matter. To do so requires a simple and highly misunderstood concept called validation. Make your clients feel understood and like they matter and you will effortlessly create a tribe of faithful followers.

Validation occurs when we confirm, mostly through words, that other people can have their own emotional experiences and we won't criticize their feelings, beliefs, or experiences in any way. A simple statement like, "It must be difficult to have something like that occur," can be very empathetic. Validation does not mean agreeing with them, or agreeing with their point of view. To validate is to reassure them that it is reasonable and okay for them to feel or think or believe the way they do – that others would probably feel similarly if the same thing happened to them. It allows your client to accept influence or advice from you simply because they feel like you understand them.

This dynamic was particularly prevalent in my client "Samantha." She came to see me with her husband and really believed that the only option left for them was divorce. Their marriage was marred by broken trust and hurt. It was during the initial session that she told me that no matter what it was I had to say, it would not make any difference to her; her mind was made up. The divorce papers were signed. She said she only came to this "stupid" intensive so that she could keep more of her money after the divorce. After listening to her and identifying key traumas that shook the relationship, I began to let her know that she was not alone... that her emotions were important and she could express her heart... that I could only imagine having so many hard circumstances happen in such a short time... and that my marriage had trekked down a treacherous path for years and at one point seemed that divorce was our only option as well. She began to listen intently as hope sparked in her heart anew. If I could re-create my marriage, so could she. And I am happy to report that she still keeps in touch. She is the first to respond to my e-mails or posts and has told numerous people about my services. Using the three keys with this client gave her the outcome she had always hoped for, and it gave me the client I always dreamed of.

2. Authenticity matters

Our society is starved for connection. We have more "friends" on social media and very few deep connections that matter. What sets an expert with a loyal following apart from the rest is the way they can make their tribe feel that they have been in their shoes. They were where the client is now, and yet they overcame. An authentic voice transcends into a person's soul, touching something deep within looking for connection. The more real and transparent you are with your audience, the deeper your connection.

Your story is the fastest way to connect with another person. Don't be afraid to share your journey. It always connects the dots for others as they plug themselves into your story. It sparks hope in another person's heart that they can get over their struggle too. When your tribe feels that you were one of them and overcame, they want to cheer you on and follow in your footsteps. But that can only happen if you are brave enough to put your own shortcomings out there.

This was so clear to me when my client "Sarah," who had severe anger and rage, came to our session particularly agitated. She was acting out until I began to tell her my story. When I let her know that I too came from an abusive background and much of my struggle came from undealt with trauma, her demeanor immediately changed. She began to identify with my story and saw the connecting pieces. This connection completely changed the course of our intensive. Authenticity has the power to connect us in a way like nothing else can.

3. Thoughts & Actions Matter

Too often we believe our thoughts without question. And yet our thought patterns and fears have held us back time and time again. By empowering your audience to not have to believe everything they think, you become the difference-maker in their lives.

You can help people re-frame their problems into opportunities, but only if they feel connected to you. Once they sense that you care, they are much more open to accepting your coaching.

Our thoughts become our words. Our words become our beliefs. Our beliefs become our actions. Our actions become our habits. Our habits become our realities. When we think whatever comes our way becomes our reality, it is real to us regardless of appearances; it is our truth. Teach others to become thought hackers by leading with your actions. Don't second-guess your instincts, which are very different than your thoughts. We allow thoughts to talk ourselves out of doing amazing things because the fear behind the thought has convinced us that we can't.

Encourage others to push past feelings. Get past those feelings to action... *"I can do it and I will!"* As soon as they have an instinct, "I should work out," or "I should go talk to my boss about that promotion," etc., have them countdown from ten and go do it without overthinking the decision or allowing fear to take the driver's seat.

If something is holding them back, encourage them to push past fear and embrace the what ifs. What if it *did* work for you? Help your clients get to the root of their block. Ask why they are experiencing the pain in their life. And keep asking the very powerful *why* question to get to the root of their limiting belief.

My client "Joey" was always second-guessing himself and sabotaging his relationships. When we questioned *why*, we were faced with the sad reality that he was always taunted and told he would always be stupid and that no one would love him. He was fulfilling that prophesy in his life, totally on autopilot. Question your own thoughts and take action to change your life and help others to do the same.

These three power keys can help you deepen your connection with your tribe and develop an audience of people who feel so united with you that they can't wait to hear from you. If you are ready to set yourself apart from the sea of coaches and consultants out there, use these techniques and begin to see just how different your outcome will be.

For more information about our intensives or services, connect with us at www.RelentlessMarriage.com and www.ReclaimMarriage.com

For access to our power packed FREE communication toolkit go to... www.RelentlessMarriage.com/toolkit

Also as a bonus we want to offer you $500 off your own personal intensive retreat. Email ReclaimMarriage@gmail.com and mention code: BEHIND THE SCENES

DIANA ASAAD

DIANA ASAAD is a crisis, intensive counselor and an award-winning author. She specializes in solution-based therapy, a type of counseling that is over 93% successful. Diana uses her many years of experience to help develop a solution-oriented plan to meet the specific needs of hurting couples to help turn their relationship around.

Diana takes great joy in guiding couples through a results-oriented process and counts it a privilege to work with each couple that comes to her. She has taken those methods and created online resources and in-person intensives to help you begin changing your relationship today!

Featured on international television and with over twenty years of ministerial service, her passion is to help lead people into transformation on every level. Diana and her husband, Hany, have three children (all girls) and they make their home in the South.

www.RelentlessMarriage.com

www.ReclaimMarriage.com

BEYOND STUCK

DR. KAZ

IF YOU'VE EVER BEEN IN A VEHICLE that got stuck in the mud or loose sand, you know the feeling of frustration. Everything you can possibly think of to attempt still leaves you stuck... until some kind stranger or super good friend comes along and pulls you out.

It's the exact same way for us mentally, except usually we aren't aware we're stuck until we're in so deeply that major symptoms occur.

I've worked with over 7731 people, helping elite and average athletes, elite and average executives – and their teams – get unstuck. What I discovered is there are three main areas of "stuckness" and one *super* area of stuckness that surfaces more today than ever before.

I've labeled the three main areas of stuckness as the H3 Hierarchy. You need to keep your *Head*, your *Heart* and your *Heinie* all in alignment. On their own, each area can be stuck, but when one or more areas are stuck, your "mental alignment" becomes out of place.

Before we check out the three main areas of stuckness, I need you to understand that our heads, hearts, and heinies are driven by what we value. There are four major types, and I like to define them as Power, Pizzazz, Precision, and Peace, because of what they value.

- *Power People* value power and control, speed, getting results quickly, moving on, and moving up.
  - Their mottos are: "Keep moving" and "Ready Fire Aim."

- *Pizzazz People* are the bling kings and queens. They live to accessorize and love creating a themed event. Not a party – a *Partay!* They value being the most stylish, super social having fun, blinging, and fun. I know I mentioned it twice, but they truly live to have twice as much fun.

  o The Pizzazzers would say: "Let's Party," or... "Ready, oh look at the flowers, the birds, I love your scarf."

- *Precision People* value numbers, data, preciseness, and perfection. They are the whiteout/rulers/spreadsheet peeps who live to find the mistakes of others.

  o Their mottos are: "Failing to Plan is Planning to Fail" and "Ready Aim, Aim, Aim, Aim."

- *Peace People* value peace and more peace. They are low-key, low-maintenance, slow moving, and loyal.

  o My Peace people would say: "Don't worry, be happy" and "Ready – What? I'm too tired to shoot anything."

The Head

One of the ways we keep ourselves stuck starts in our head. The *Head* area deals with our *truths*. If you struggle to tell yourself the truth or to tell others the truth, this is an area of stuckness – personally, departmentally, and even organizationally.

To find out your unique level of stuckness, visit
www.GoBeyondStuck.com/areasofstuckness
now for a quick survey.

Three of the four personalities struggle with the telling the truth 100 percent of the time – so that means at least 75 percent of the population struggles with telling the truth. But remember, that means they struggle with it, but some will fight through to tell most of the truth... or at least what needs to be known... or possibly just their version of the truth.

Over the decades I've added new ways to teach yourself, your family, and your team/tribe to consistently and easily tell the truth without butchering someone's feelings. Three of my favorites are:

1. Track what you tell yourself and how often you lie. It goes something like this: Tomorrow at 6:00 A.M. I'll run/walk/go to the gym/meditate… but you don't. Instead, "Mr. Excuse" drops by for a visit.

2. Have two Truth Days a week where you must tell the truth for 24 hours, both to yourself and everyone around you. Sound easy? Wait till a co-worker asks how you like their new recipe for sugar-free/dairy-free/gluten-free/fat-free and flavor-free kale muffins. Good luck!

3. Start your team/family meetings with three truths. This is my take on the game of "two truths and a lie." You must tell three truths that compliment everyone in the circle. This trains you to compliment while observing what others do well. If you're a Power Peep, this will really stretch your ability to compliment and tell the truth. For a greater list, check out www.GoBeyondStuck.com/TruthActivities

I remember working with a professional baseballer in Australia who constantly told himself how poorly he played, and mentally beat himself up for errors at first base. I explained to him when he "lied" to himself, he was pummeling his self-confidence as well as having a conversation in his head that really screwed his teammates. He needed to be switched on all the time at first base and if an error occurred, he was to forget it and forge ahead, reminding himself he was a dedicated teammate who consistently kept his mind on the game and his job at first base.

Lies transfer into business, sports and even schools. Blaming/shaming/condemnation of who we are or what we do is simply a *lie* we tell ourselves. Some personalities are more likely to "lie" to themselves through shame and blame. I remember working with an entire executive team in a bakery who were all family members. Although everyone knew someone was stealing product and selling to other bakeries, no one wanted to address the elephant in the room. They decided to just "pretend" the theft did not occur to avoid embarrassment and "keep the family happy." Telling the truth may be a slippery slide, however, to get unstuck in your Head, it's a must.

The Heart

The second area of stuckness is discovered in your *Heart*. This area is much more subtle than your Head. When you get stuck in your Heart you are suffering from a lack of trust: in yourself, the ones you love, your friends, or your team members. Lack of trust usually starts with doubt. In sport this may show up as doubting you've chosen the "right club" or doubting you and your horse will clear the four-foot, six-inch jump. In business, I see the doubt/lack of trust surface as consistently micro-managing team members, checking and rechecking numbers/contracts/details.

As the world population becomes more heart-centered, this area of stuckness has grown just as our lack of trust in ourselves and others grows. Only one of the four main personalities trusts naturally, so learning to trust from your Head and Heart is a learned skill.

One of the best ways to develop trust is through mental and physical exercise. I remember working with a professional baseball team who lacked trust in each other and themselves. They'd had a horrible previous season, placing last in the league. I recommended a high ropes course and scheduled it for an upcoming Saturday. I was new to the coaching staff and decided not to ride the bus with the guys. When I arrived at the high ropes facility, they had already started their instruction on how to work the course. As I watched their fears surface, I noticed the jokes started to increase. Then one of them called out, "Hey Sigmund (my nickname after Sigmund Freud), you need to be doing this with us!"

My heart froze. My fear of heights was unnaturally strong, and I immediately said I was there to observe, not participate. Then it became a pack mentality as all 22 men cajoled and taunted me. I finally gave in and got strapped into the harness. Needless to say, the trust in myself to accomplish the first task was below zero and almost caused me to quit. However, the team knew I was panicking and began to joke with me, talk to me, help me take my mind off the fear and trust that I did know what to do next. What started as distrust in myself to conquer a fear became one of the most empowering days in my life – all because of 22 baseballers who needed to bond with each other, but wound up helping me discover that I could trust myself and them.

Three of my favorite trust-building activities are:

1. Conquering an internal fear. It does not need to be huge – fear of taking a transit bus somewhere, fear or speaking in front of others, fear of learning to line dance. Whatever you choose, decide if you need to do this alone or with a cheerleader or an entire squad of cheerleaders.

2. Start planning for success. Create a vision, mission statements, and goals – an action plan for your steps to success. Trust starts with holding yourself accountable.

3. I love a team trust-building activity that's easy to implement and involves both mental and physical challenges, so those who trust their intelligence win and those who trust their strength win.

For a greater list of Trust activities check out
www.GoBeyondStuck.com/TrustActivities

The Heinie

Although everyone laughs when I talk about the area of stuckness in the *Heinie*, this is the area where you take action, or as I like to say, "get traction!" I'm not referring to movement. I mean action that has quantifiable results. When you get stuck here, you go into inaction/analysis of paralysis/non-stop planning – any excuse to do something that looks active, yet has little to no measurable results in the project you are currently working on.

One of my favorite avoidance tactics when I'm writing is to clean my home – crazy clean my home. The cleaning is a movement that produces a result, because I love how clean my house is, however it is not the measurable result of pages written.

What's your go-to avoidance activity? In the corporate world we call it "being busy." In reality, it's better to be focused and effective than busy with non-stop movement.

I remember a banking client that was so proud of its huge sales center room where everyone sat at open desks – no walls, no privacy, no way to focus. In a company-wide needs analysis, it was brought up that there was zero time to accomplish any of their daily tasks because phones rang nonstop. Employees were falling further and further behind because of the constant phone interruptions.

I asked what they did with their phone during lunch or when they went to the bathroom. They said they forwarded the calls to a teammate. Then I asked if each of the 40 of them – five at a time – could forward their calls for one hour a day, and put on headsets to block out the noise.

What a difference that made! The focused power hour allowed them to complete more work in one hour than they had been accomplishing in a whole day, and the peacefulness lowered their stress.

Intentional action = focused, concentrated, deliberate

How does this area of stuckness appear in athletes? I've seen it when an athlete works out or practices in their best/most favorite area because it's easy and fun – often neglecting the "challenging parts" of their sport. They might also travel from event to event appearing to be "active" yet consistently getting the same results, without looking outside of the events for additional coaching to improve their skills. This stuckness also may appear as amazing sporting results in practice rounds but then a complete disaster round during competition or tournaments.

Three of my favorite action/traction activities are:

1. Start small and repeatable for 17 days. If you need to improve putting, do 23 minutes of putting for 17 days. If you need to build to running 53 miles per week, add a quarter-mile a day for 17 days. Or if you need to stretch more, stretch during the commercials of your favorite TV show for 17 days.

2. I love Mel Robbins' Five-Second Rule – count backwards from five to one, and then just do it.

3. Have a reward system in place. Set mini-goals and reward yourself all along the way. When you reach mini-goal 1, perhaps it's seven minutes of dancing to your favorite song, or seven minutes of escape into an audio book. The bigger the goal or closer you get to the finish line, the larger the reward should be. Make it fun and easy to do, and involve others in your joy whenever possible.

For a more amazing ideas on action/traction activities check out
www.GoBeyondStuck.com/TractionActivities

I did not discover the last area of stuckness until I got so trapped in it, it almost destroyed me. It's an area of stuckness where there is a disconnect between your head and your heart. It's a lie we tell ourselves with statements like "That's not like me," "I'm not into the mushy stuff," "I'm not a hand holder," or "My job is to get things done, not make friends..." It's an avoidance technique to not become fully invested in something with both your Head and your Heart. And I know right now, my devout *Power People* are thinking "Wait a minute, I don't do that 'heart' stuff. I was right there with you – until..."

My BFF, Beryl, was dying from lymphoma – her third round with this hideous killer. I had decided to move from Australia back to the U.S. in June of 1998 after living there for 10 years and would be back to Australia to finalize everything in two weeks. Beryl was throwing me a small going away party in her living room and as I stood to leave she stood up and opened her arms to me. We were not the hugging type so it was a bit weird, but I knew she wanted and needed a hug. So I stepped in to hug her. She pulled me in for what I call a DGH – death grip hug. She held on so tightly for so long. When I finally started to pull away, she whispered something in my ear.

"Don't go."

What? Don't go! This trip had been planned for six months and I'd be back in two weeks. We could say a proper goodbye then. I made a joke about how we'd go surfing when I returned. Without another word, Beryl let go. But her eyes were begging me to stay.

Five days after I left, I got the call in my Denver hotel room that Beryl had been put into a drug-induced coma to alleviate her pain. Two days later they woke her up to say goodbye to her family, and that night she had a stroke and died.

I have never cried so much in my life. Hours of just sobbing on the hotel bed, angry that I hadn't taken the time to properly say goodbye, to tell her how much I loved her, and how special she was to me. That was the third time in my life I had a chance to get past a lifetime of stuckness... but I had failed again. It took me almost five years to come to terms and break through that huge area of personal stuckness.

One of my favorite quotes is: "How you do anything is how you do everything!" That's why small actionable steps to moving through your areas stuckness are far greater than grandiose actions which are hard to consistently repeat.

Now, every time I want to disconnect from a difficult Heart situation, I remember Beryl's last words to me. *"Don't go."*

So my message to you today is: *"Don't go..."* one more day being stuck. *"Don't go..."* one more week without helping those around you to get unstuck. And *"Don't go..."* one more month denying your greatness to the world!

To discover how to get unstuck right now visit
www.GoBeyondStuck.com/course

DR. KAZ

DR. KAZ is an award-winning international speaker, author, and coach who has worked with Fortune 100 companies, international associations, 3 Olympic teams and 34 Olympians from the U.S., Australia, and Pacific Rim. She's known to many throughout the world as the "Gitter Done Gal."

Dr. KAZ works with movers and shakers and impact makers on getting unstuck and teaching how to live in "Competitive Balance – where intensity meets inner peace and momentum explodes." When you're seeking more power, passion, pizzazz, and peace that impacts your productivity and profits – call KAZ.

She'll make everyone a believer in "Ask a great question and you'll always get a *great* answer!" She enlightens and empowers audiences to challenge what is, change what is not working, and champion causes that impact the greater good. In her own words, "I work with people who want to *be* more and organizations that want to *do* more." KAZ lives by her credo – "I'd rather wear out than rust out!"

You are either an influencer or being influenced
– the choice is always yours!...

What's Stopping You
From Your Secure Retirement

In 20 Minutes a Day

Dr. Fred Rouse

PEOPLE WORK FOR 20-30 YEARS OR MORE trying to accumulate enough money for their retirement. They know there's no way they can save enough. They know they need to do something to make that money grow.

For the vast majority, the default action is to invest in the stock market in some way, shape, or form. They have a company-sponsored 401K, a 403b, or some other work-related deferred compensation plan they contribute to from payroll withholding. They may have an IRA, a Roth IRA, or if self-employed maybe a SEP. But other than their homes, these retirement funds represent the majority of their wealth.

Nearly *all* of that money ends up in the stock market.

Yet even with all that, studies show that 56% of Americans have less than $10,000 saved for retirement.

There is a way out. It's not too late. You can still save your retirement.

Many people will tell you that if you're at the halfway point or older and don't already have at least the bare minimum of $850k in savings that it's too late for you. I'm here to tell you, it's *not* too late. You can still have the retirement that you want and deserve even if you only have as little as $10,000 in savings today.

But don't wait any longer! At this point, time is *not* on your side. I can show you how to make more money, but I can't show you how to make more time.

It took me 10 years of research and over $350k of my own money to develop a system specifically for people ages 50 and older to generate sufficient cash flow so they can retire in just 3-5 years.

In my program (Short Window Retirement Planning), I show people how to generate a predictable income in less than 20 minutes a day just 2-3 times a month that is *not* dependent on the stock market or the economy in general. Only a very small part of your account is in the market for a maximum of just 4 days at a time.

I was talking to Jean and Rick from Riverside, CA, a few weeks ago. Rick retired at age 56 with a very healthy seven-figure nest egg. He's 68 years old now. When the stock market crashed in 2008 he lost 43% of his money. He went into a full blown panic and invested the money he had left with "friends" that he knew for over 25 years that were very experienced in their own businesses. He ended up losing the rest of his money and pulled it out when he was down to $1,200.

Jean and Rick spent the next few years downsizing and saving every penny of a small pension they had. They were living month to month. They were both pretty depressed but determined not to accept what looked like their fate. Rick kept looking for something. He saw me on the internet and what I was saying seemed to grab and hold his attention. He scheduled a call. We spoke. And later that night he contacted me and wanted to get involved. He knew that it was the last best chance he had to save his retirement. He emailed me this comment.

> "When the stock market plunged in 2008 I lost 43% of the equity in my retirement portfolio I was depressed but determined to not accept my fate. I was watching a YouTube video when Dr. Fred appeared on the screen. I found myself absorbed with what he was saying. I now feel optimistic again, invigorated and determined to restart a fulfilling retirement. Thank you Dr. Fred."

This is someone who did everything right. He had well over $1M dollars and got wiped out at the *first* market crash in his retirement. At 68 he'll have at least one more. Possibly two more market crashes while he's in retirement. He and Jean are both in really good health. However, *now* when those crashes happen they'll be basically unaffected because their cash flow will be independent of the markets.

Here's Billy Ray. He's 67, living in Indiana. He had his own business for a while; it crashed and burned with a bad turn of the economy. He worked various jobs over the years and when I was on a call with him, he told me he was day trading a 9-minute chart from 8:30 a.m. until 12:30 p.m. every day before he did his six-hour shift at Lowes. What that means is that he can't leave his computer screen from 8:30 in the morning until after noon time every day. Every 9 minutes he gets a new chart on the screen and he has to make constant trading decisions the entire time. He's 67. That's a lot of stress, and he would have been happy making just $100-$200/month because most day traders lose money.

I didn't get him out of Lowes yet but we did save him 20 hours a week since he quit day trading and he's well on his way to leaving Lowes too. This is what he wrote:

> "I was day trading 4 hours a day, and barely making any money, and then I went to do my six-hour shift at Lowes. Then I talked to Dr Fred. He made all the difference and turned my life around."

So what can we learn? In both of these situations these folks thought they were doing everything right. They thought they were prepared. However outside factors, over which they had no control, upended and basically destroyed their lives.

Building their savings to over 7 figures and having their own business didn't work for these folks.

While they were going along and things were working out okay for them, Rick and Jean and Billy Ray had a misplaced hope that things would just continue along that path and they'd continue to be okay.

However, when things turned bad – and they always do at some point – they quickly realized they didn't have any real control over their money or the economy in general.

So what do we do?

First let's ditch the fallacy of having $1.2M to 1.5M dollars in retirement savings. That 30-year plan, where you put in $1000/month for 30 years to buy and hold various stocks, mutual funds and annuities, just hasn't worked for you... by a lot!

...and now you're looking around trying to figure out what went wrong and how you could possibly fix at least enough of it, so you don't have to be working into your 70s and beyond just to barely survive.

...you lay in bed at night and wonder if there is some way you could make some more money or have your money making more money ...or maybe *both!*

There's only so much time, and if you work a second or third job, is it really going to make a substantial difference in your retirement savings?

Is that remotely what you want to be doing at this point in your life?

That money in your retirement plan is only there to generate cash flow that you can live on. If the market takes a hit, so does your cash flow.

Second, if you have a small business that's grossing under 7 figures a year, chances are that if the economy turns, you're going to take a hit too. On top of that, can you/do you want to still be operating that business well into your 70s and beyond? Probably not.

The goal for you is to first decide what *you want to be doing in your retirement years.* Retirement is not sitting in a rocking chair just waiting to die.

In my best-selling book, *Cracking the Code to Success* that's co-authored with Brian Tracy – the international businessman that taught Tony Robbins and Jack Canfield, I define retirement as:

> "Retirement is being able to do what you want, experience and maintain the lifestyle you want, without worrying about the money."

Once we decide what we want to do in retirement, now we need to figure out how much cash flow we'll need on an annual basis to pay for it.

Unlike the "retirement calculators" that everyone who is failing uses, this is simpler than most people think.

For most of those I talk with, they'll need to at least equal the income they are earning before retirement. To have a safe cushion, you'll probably need *an average 125% of what you're making pre-retirement.*

So HOW do we get that cash flow for our retirement?

We've identified the 6 things that are in the way of our progress. They are:

1. Structural Issues

It's generally not your fault. There are structural issues built into the system that are preventing you from really getting ahead.

Wall Street, the government, the politicians, and the bankers have rigged the system so they get most all of the breaks. It's been that way since Reagan took office. Trickle-down economics have *never*, and will *never* trickle down to you

2. Lack of Proper Knowledge for *Your* Current Situation

The 30-year plan. You don't have 30 years to put $1000/month away and wait for it to grow. That is, if it grows and doesn't get wiped out like it did in 2008 when the market took a 43% hit (and for some people it didn't come back to break-even as of today, depending on what you were invested in).

3. Lack of a Plan for *Your* Current Situation

You're 50+. You've been on this same plan for the last 20-30 years. You've been trying to put some money into the company 401k or your IRA. There never seems to be enough and then you had that emergency and you had to pull some of it out. What a surprise, it never got put back.

You've been busy with life. Things happen, a wedding, a divorce, the car broke down, you get hospitalized for just a couple of days and there's an $80k bill that's *not* covered by your insurance.

4. Lack of Decision

You're feeling like Alice in Wonderland when she asks the cat, "Which road should I take?" The response: "If you don't know where you want to end up, it doesn't matter."

Without knowing where we want to wind up, it's impossible to develop a plan and make a decision.

5. Lack of Consistent Action

Life happens along the way and no matter what our best intentions were at the time, we seem to have a problem, sometimes not of our own making, to take consistent action to follow through on the decisions that we make once we actually make them.

6. Lack of a Mentor

Did you ever notice that *every* great sports figure has a personal trainer? Or that every sports team has a coach who guides the players on the field?

Why is that? Because an objective third party who knows the sport or game can help the players fix the little things that can make them stars in their fields.

How do we overcome them or negate the effect of these 6 roadblocks to get our end result – an Ultimate Secure Retirement – at an age young enough that we can still enjoy it?

To be honest there's little that we can do with our time and resources that is going to make any meaningful change in our lifetimes for our retirement to the structural issues.

The past has happened. We can try to learn from it, however we can only live in today and we don't want to waste the short window of time we have worrying about what may or may not happen tomorrow.

There is an interesting interplay with the remaining 5 things that you can affect which are preventing you from getting more money for your retirement.

First you need to find out where you are today

Get the correct Knowledge for *you* to develop the proper Plan for your specific situation.

You need your Plan so you can make a decision or decisions in order to take Action.

Because you have only a short window of time to turn things around, you need a Mentor or a Coach to cut through all the nonsense out there and guide you in a systematic way to the Correct Knowledge for Your Current Situation.

Finding out where you're at in your retirement planning situation tends to be a bit more challenging than you may think.

Did you ever notice that before they had GPS and smart phones with maps that sometimes you could be driving and driving?

Someone told you where to go and how to get there. You thought you were following the directions and then you noticed that nothing looked familiar. You were not where you were supposed to be.

So too with retirement planning; you can go online at over a dozen different sites and find "retirement calculators."

If you're 50+ and you don't already have close to $900k, each and every one of them is going to tell you basically the same thing. You're screwed.

They tell you that because they were all set up by the financial "professional" who wants you to work on the only plan they know. It's the 30-year $1,000/month buy-and-hold plan that hasn't worked for you to date.

They have no idea how to help in your specific situation – 50+ with an underfunded retirement account.

And now that you're 50+ and have a very short window of time to get something to work for you, that plan works even less. So what do you do?

Before you do anything else you need to find out where you actually are in your journey to your Ultimate Secure Retirement. How do you do that?

I've been working with clients and students for over 30 years and noticed that every one of them has this same problem. They know where they came from financially. They know the spot where they want and need to end up – their Ultimate Secure Retirement.

And they know how much they're making today.

They have a very difficult time finding where all the pieces fit together and how to overcome the 5 things that are preventing them from getting to their goal.

I developed The REAL Money Doctor's "Ultimate Secure Retirement Roadmap."

In it, I show you how to determine exactly where you are in your journey to your Ultimate Secure Retirement.

It covers what knowledge you need to move to the next level of your journey as well as how much debt and savings are at each level and step of the way.

It shows you how to get to the point of zero debt and sufficient cash flow, even starting at age 50+.

This is an invaluable resource to help you locate exactly where you're at and the steps needed to move you closer to your Ultimate Secure Retirement.

Because you obviously have an interest in securing your retirement by reading this section of this book, I'd like to offer this invaluable guide, the "Ultimate Secure Retirement Roadmap" to you at no cost.

Download your free copy at
DrRouseNow.com/ROADMAP

DR. FRED ROUSE

DR. FRED ROUSE, CFP (aka: The REAL Money Doctor) is the top Certified Financial Planner®, Money Expert, and International Best-Selling Author who has received several national awards for his writing and money expertise.

He is the nation's top expert on Short Window Retirement Planning. It's the only program developed specifically for the unique needs of people 50 and older so they can have their Ultimate Secure Retirement in just 3–5 years starting with as little as $10K today.

His mission is to help people Get, Protect, and Enjoy their Money, Life, and Retirement. He hosts *The REAL Money Doctor Show* on his YouTube channel where he shows people how to live their worry-free Ultimate Secure Retirement.

Dr. Rouse and his work have been featured on FOX News, ABC, NBC, CBS, CNN, CNBC, *USA Today*, Forbes, *Wall Street Journal*, *Newsweek*, *Inc Magazine*, and more. To learn more about Dr. Rouse and how he can help you and your retirement, contact him directly at (215) 646-1170, DrRouse@DrFredRouse.com or visit DrFredRouse.com.

Customer Service... Who Cares?

Howard Globus

WHO LIKES BEING IGNORED? Anyone?

Whether it's not being able to catch the bartender's attention, having the couple who came in the restaurant after you be noticed and seated first, or going into a cell phone store for a frustrating problem that should have been taken care of remotely, we want to be acknowledged and treated with respect.

But who cares about customer service? Let's be honest with each other. I know how much I love calling the insurance company and being asked to key in my account number, date of birth, social security number, and maybe my shoe size to get into a phone tree, then have to verbally answer more automated questions, reconfirm some of that same information only to get routed to a representative who asks me... the exact same information to "confirm" my account.

So, how are you treating *your* prospects and customers? Are they dialing your main office number to press "1" for sales, "2" for support (which, by the way, implies that I'm more important if I'm calling to buy something rather than asking for help with something I've already bought), and then maybe finally getting routed around to a live person who will still need to connect the customer to you as the owner?

How It Begins

Most entrepreneurs first start business with knowledge from the technician role. I don't mean that you start out as a mechanic or someone who takes physical things apart and puts them back together. I mean you are a coach or a florist or an application developer or an accountant or a lawyer who does the work.

What you are doing is the *technical* aspect of the business. You *are* the coach or the florist or application developer or accountant or lawyer. You are good at the thing you are doing.

Because you want to help more people (and earn more money), you feel that you can do it better and with more joy if you open your own business. So you hang out a shingle and do the technical work – the thing you are good at. Your business starts to grow by word of mouth, or through advertising, or both. Your customers see that you know what you're doing and that you are good at it... and they refer other people.

You probably give out your direct or cell phone number to your prospects and customers. Everyone is thrilled with the personal service they receive. But how well does that work as you grow from five customers to twenty or a hundred? Nice problem to have, but still a problem.

Scaling Up

Anyone who has been in business for a bit of time knows about "feast or famine." As a technician, you can handle work that comes in – as long as it is planned and in the right volume. When there isn't enough work, you must network, market, advertise, build blogs and so on. But as you attract attention and get noticed, the work piles on and you might stop the building aspects so you can turn to doing the technical job.

When looking for customers to build your business, customer service is critical. The first phone call or email interaction can make the difference between losing a sale and creating a lifelong customer.

Even today, although a large percentage of commerce is done via email and webpage sales forms, answering the business phones is critical. New customers want to know there is a real business behind what they are buying. They may have questions about the product or service that you are selling, or there may be a slight difference in package A or package B. Often times that first phone call is to gauge whether the person on the other end of the line is someone they want to do business with – someone they will trust with their personal information.

When a prospect or customer calls your business, they are already primed and engaged, looking to find someone of a like mind on the other end of the phone. If the call rings and no one answers it – or if it is answered by an auto-attendant – many time the dialer will hang up and go down the Google search results to contact the next company on the list.

If you are doing any kind of marketing – web, email, postcard or smoke signals – if you *paid* to make that phone ring and yet you do not answer it, that money is lost, never to be recovered.

Whenever I have a challenge getting a new vendor or supplier on the phone, the question that always goes through my mind is: "If it's this hard to get them on the phone when I want to *give* them my money, how hard will it be to get them to respond when I have a problem and need assistance?"

The frustration and annoyance I experience when I am buying something reminds me to revisit my own customer support processes and experiences. Are *my* prospects feeling the same way when they reach out to *my* company? Where can I remove impediments to help these new people come and experience the excellent work that my business does?

Even worse, when I view the problems that my customers have in getting in touch with someone in my business – hopefully, the person who can solve their problem – I must take a long look and ask: "Is my business treating customers the way that I would want to be treated?"

It's well established that selling to current or recent customers is significantly less expensive than prospecting new business. Current and past customers already know, like, and trust us and have seen the benefit of using the service or products we are selling. Providing excellent customer service is a universal goal which is rarely met as businesses grow.

Setting the Mood

Answering a business phone live and promptly sets up a different kind of customer service. The voice that speaks for your business can establish a more positive experience for your customer.

What kind of brand or experience are you looking to impart? Whimsical and fun, stoic and serious, earnest and helpful? You wouldn't want someone like Annie Potts from the 1984 movie *Ghostbusters* answering the phone at your headquarters with the equivalent of "Ghostbusters, whaddaya want?"

If we look at two fictional companies – Fred's Finances and Murray's Money Managers – we can get a view of what type of mood is set in a customer's first interaction over the phone.

Both businesses provide financial services to their customers with a focus on managing a small business' cash flow, payroll, taxes, and providing planning and retirement services to its owners. Both companies are themselves small businesses that have been owned and operated for over twenty years by the same individuals. Each business has a staff of four, plus the owner, who take great pride in providing financially sound advice to ensure that their customers can retire comfortably when the customer is ready.

Fred's Finances has put in a new phone system with an "auto-attendant," that recorded voice that says, "Thank you for calling Fred's Finances. If you would like to speak with a sales representative, press 1. If you would like to speak with a billing specialist press 2. If you are a current customer and would like assistance, please press 3." Fred's thought was that most of his employees are out in the field every day working at customer sites and it would be a good way to route calls to provide better customer service. The auto-attendant forwards all calls – regardless of the option chosen – to someone's cell phone so that no matter where the employees are, the call will get answered.

Murray's Money Managers also has a new phone system in place where calls can be routed to the appropriate associate because, like Fred's people, most are out at customer sites during the regular workday. Murray, however, chose to have an outside service answer the phone live, then route calls to the person best able to address a specific problem or project. The service cost one-eighth the price of his lowest paid employee, without added benefits or payroll tax expenses. When a prospect calls Murray's Money Managers, the greeting they receive from a human is: "Hello, thank you for calling Murray's Money Managers. This is Chris speaking. How can I help you?" Based on the questions asked or who the caller would like to speak with, Chris then forwards the call directly to the correct person's cell phone. If that person is not available, the message does not go into voicemail. Instead, Chris picks the caller back up and asks 3–5 specific questions, then lets the caller know the person they would like to speak with will call them back. Chris then fills out a web form and a message gets sent by text and emailed to the person who needs to return the call. A daily report is generated for Murray to review, to ensure customers' needs are being addressed.

Fred's system answers the call and has callers self-direct to the appropriate extension. But what happens if someone calls and has two questions – one a support question and one a billing question? Which extension will they dial? And those who rarely call Fred's main number forget that they can just press 3 to get to customer service, so they have to wait through the 10- or 15-second auto-attendant. In a world where we already feel disconnected, it's natural for someone to wonder if anyone will really listen to their voicemail... and who knows how long until they get a call back?

Murray's phone system is set up with the idea that when someone calls, people want to talk to people, and they would rather not figure out if they need to press 1 for this or 2 for that. They simply want to be heard... and helped. With a live operator answering, that feeling can be generated. In addition, there is a system to ensure that messages are sent in multiple formats, and someone with a vested interest – Murray, the owner – will be checking to make sure the messages will be followed up.

Capturing the Info

Next, it's a good idea to know what information should be gathered from these phone calls. As a one-person shop, whether the call is from a customer or a prospect, you need to keep track of what information was shared, and when the caller was promised you would get back to them.

If you're not the person answering the phone, it is even more important to establish what information should be captured and relayed to resolve the caller's issues. This information can then be used to screen or route the call to someone who can actually *help*, which is the whole point of answering the phone live anyway.

As mentioned above, Fred's system relies on the caller to self-determine where the call should be routed. And the amount of information that is left sometimes ends up being: "Hey, this is Steve. I'm having a problem... call me back right away." This leaves too much ambiguity. Steve who? The caller did not leave a phone number and there are seven customers on file named Steve or Steven or Stephen. With caller ID and call stamp, it can be deduced, but it adds time and steps to the process and slows down the speed of reply. Also, we don't know what problem Steve is having. Maybe payroll didn't run, the taxes weren't sent, a lien notice came in, the 401K payment wasn't made, or perhaps an employee was found siphoning funds. It's a crap shoot who should call back to resolve Steve's issue in one call. In this case, it would be best if Fred calls because he is the owner and can direct the correct action, not knowing what the initial request will be.

Murray's system removes some of the guesswork. When Chris is gathering information, she is captures the name of the caller, the phone number, the best time to return the call, who the caller thinks they want to speak with and the nature of the call/problem. This information allows Chris to learn how to route the call. Murray can later review and confirm that the calls are being routed correctly. And if the customer has a billing question but also needs to speak with someone about payroll, messages can be sent to both associates to call the customer back, with the information in hand to help.

Be Intentional

What outcome do you want your prospect or customer to have from the call? If this is not determined prior to answering the phone, your prospect or customer will be the one who sets the tone and intentionality.

From a business owner's perspective, that can be very dangerous. Someone calling to complain or demanding to speak to the owner may be instantly calmed and put at ease when the phone is answered in a calm, polite manner.

For an entrepreneur wearing all the business hats, it can be overwhelming to take calls while trying to provide the work product. Knowing how the caller should be greeted and what frame of mind you are looking to have them in is key. Someone is controlling the call; shouldn't it be you?

Fred's business is reacting to the call, scrambling to handle the interaction as a cold hand-off because the auto-attendant doesn't know if the caller is a prospect or a customer, happy or upset, has many questions or just one. The recipient is caught at an immediate disadvantage by having no frame of reference for the conversation. That can be exciting, but it can also produce anxiety and less responsiveness from staff, especially when in the middle of working on a process or project at another customer's site.

Murray's business fields the call with an idea of what the caller needs... before they get on the phone because Chris can mention that the caller sounds upset and the associate can be prepared on how to address the situation. If information is gathered by Chris for a return call, the associate can control the flow of the conversation and have information ready to answer potential questions. Chris can set the intention that the caller's issue or problem *will* be addressed and that an associate *will* be calling back within twenty minutes (or whatever the desired timing is) to work with the caller, setting the caller's expectations about when to expect a return call and that the associate returning the call will actually be prepared to address what the caller is asking about.

Checking In

When your business grows to a point where a virtual assistant or receptionist is hired, how can you guarantee the phone experience is what you are looking to create for your callers?

The only way to ensure that the proper tone, information gathering, and intentional experience is taking place is by monitoring some calls. Live or recordings, business owners should be checking in periodically that what is happening is what they want to happen. If it isn't, training or changes need to be made.

As Fred hires an assistant, he needs to first come up with a script and process to answer calls. Fred hasn't worried about calls being returned before, or how they have been handled with his auto-attendant system and he is just now starting to learn of how differently his associates handle the phone calls.

Murray has been using his system for a while and receives reports on the messages coming in. He can spot-check with customers that their questions are being answered. Murray has listened to recordings of how Chris interacts with callers and made modifications over time to tweak the process and ensure the correct information get gathered and that it's done in a professional way that isn't too stiff.

Follow Through

What needs to happen once the call is complete? Without an intentional process, your paid advertising that makes the phones ring will be money lost.

There does not need to be anything robotic about this process. Knowing your customer's journey is helpful. Knowing your sales process is a good place to start to build the follow-up processes to make certain that calls result in good customer service and experiences.

Ultimately when customers and prospects are treated well with intention, and in a way we would like to be treated, it will establish respect and trust from which you can grow quality, loyal customer relationships. Doing this consistently and with intentionality will become part of a business' DNA when there is a process to follow. Interactions do not and should not be scripted, but it helps to have a road map of how interactions should flow to the intended outcomes in order to provide a consistent, quality experience.

See our list of the first 10 questions to ask
when building your process:

buildyourcustomerserviceprocess.com

or phonestuff.guru/10qs

HOWARD GLOBUS

HOWARD GLOBUS is a Security Evangelist and a passionate proponent of customer service to build a successful business. Through carefully cultivating and nurturing a small but loyal client base he was able to recover from the cratering of his first business to rebuild a resilient and successful seven-figure business.

Shifting Into the Fast Lane: Your Highway to Success

Jennifer Carman

LOOKING FOR STRONGER PERSONAL AND PROFESSIONAL RELATIONSHIPS? How do you know what the core issue is, and how do you release the blocks that are holding you back from ultimate success in these relationships? Why even bother in the first place?

The answer is less complicated than you might think. There are a few rules of the mind – call them "expert secrets" – that can shift massive obstacles in your life. I'm going to share them with you here, and in less time than you think, you'll have immediate access to shift past roadblocks, allowing the roadmaps of the success highway to open up to you, in the fast lane no less.

Hello, fortunate one! I'm Jennifer Carman, the Pineapple Parenting Coach. For over 15 years I've been helping people worldwide, not just parents, shift perspectives by easily getting to the root of major blocks in a compassionate way with as much humor as possible. Humor is key. When we're dealing with major life changes and upheaval, sometimes it's impossible to find a reason to smile... let alone laugh. But when we can use humor as a tool to deal with the hard stuff, we find deeper meaning and a joy in life again. I was born with this gift and I share it by helping others, which brings me even more joy. More smiles on more faces – the planet could use more of that, right? Yes!

Having written books, traveled worldwide teaching workshops and helped clients massively shift and heal major blocks in their lives, I love what I do and provide results that bring such great relief to people.

Why does getting to the root/core matter? When you plant a garden, you need to tend to it – nurture it, water it, feed it sunshine and maybe fertilizer. You must also weed it properly. If not, the weeds will take over and kill off the beautiful fruits, veggies, and flowers you worked so hard to grow. Green thumb gardeners know that if you don't get those weeds out all the way to the root, they come back with a vengeance. You must not only get to the root, but remove it fully to make sure it's gone for good.

It's the same with our blocks and issues in life. We can band-aid things, applying superficial ointment to mask or tolerate symptoms. Sometimes we need that to just get by. But, if you want to totally transform something, like a caterpillar into a butterfly, you need to be able to get to the actual cause or root of that issue – the *real* cause, not the superficial symptom. The wisdom, healing, clearing, and transformation that come from doing just that gives you a tremendous leap forward in whatever you may be struggling with.

You have parents, or people who raised you, no matter whether they were your biological parents. Those primary caregivers who were responsible for you from birth to about six years of age had more influence on you than you or they may have ever realized. If you currently have children, especially infants to teens, you can not only transform the blocks you are carrying from your own childhood, but learn techniques that will prevent unknowingly and unintentionally passing those same issues onto your kids. It's a *win-win*!

A childhood full of memories is what you may have, and many of them may be positive and joyful. If you think of the number of days you've been alive, however, there are lots and lots of memories you can't recall, especially if some weren't so positive. Those memories get sent away because they are simply too intense to process or deal with in the moment. Actually, it's those memories that get suppressed and resurface unexpectedly, then cause turmoil in our lives years later. However, healing usually occurs when those suppressed memories are dealt with. Then, miracles happen and life becomes magical again.

How you felt about those experiences played more of a part, and continues to play a part in your life, no matter if someone else has a different opinion of the circumstances. Our perception of what happened to us as young children – and the emotions evoked during any given experience – are what contribute to the unconscious lifelong patterns that may be inhibiting our ultimate success, both personally and professionally.

"It's all in your head..." Heard this one? Maybe you've said it to others, and maybe it's been said to you. While having some truth, it is not the whole truth. We've been mistakenly sold on the notion that if something is simply "in your head" then you can self-talk or positively affirm your way out of it... and you may be able to do this with some success for a certain amount of time. However, if it's a deep issue – let's call it a subconscious pattern or belief – it will keep rearing its ugly head until it's dealt with at the roots. Or it will continue to wreak havoc on aspects of your life while you run in circles trying to deal with it over and over again.

In my first book, *Solace 7*, I speak about how dealing with things at their root is where we create major transformation.

Where do your resilience and strength, confidence and motivation come from? Do you call upon a higher power in times of need, whether that be God, or universe, or universal oneness, or a religious deity?

I had been zipping along in my life, quite independent, owning a business I opened during my last semester of college. Talk about motivated! Prior to that I ran an on-site corporate wellness center for Verizon Wireless. I loved helping people, whether it was physical, emotional, or spiritual wellness. I was using my gifts and life was grand.

Then came an experience that changed my life forever. It was a catalyst in my deep dive, personal spiritual journey. I gave birth to a beautiful amazing baby after a full-term, normal healthy pregnancy... but then had to make the decision of taking him off life support about a week later.

I was left with a hole in my heart that I thought would never heal. A year later, on the anniversary of his death – and my birthday as well – I was three months pregnant and miscarried. I sat staring at the wall in the doctor's office and asked to be left alone. The nurse came in and said, "Good news, bad news." It didn't seem at the time that there was any chance of any news being "good," but I told her to just lay it on me. Well yes, there was in fact a miscarriage but it was a "clean" one and wouldn't require further medical intervention. The body did what it was supposed to do when something wasn't working right.

I'm going to repeat that last statement because it's got depth of wisdom. "The body did what it was supposed to do when something wasn't working right."

How many times do we fight against what happens? We bypass our feelings and emotions and go straight to our heads, psycho-analyzing our situations and others in our lives.

The biggest most important aspect to growth and movement is actually acceptance. But *acceptance* is not *settling*. It's not saying that we should accept situations which are unhealthy or inhibiting our growth and potential. Acceptance is just a step that is most often bypassed. If we would only put more faith and trust into life and the infinite wisdom all around us, we would open the doors to soar high and fly free.

I could have stayed stuck in the tragic story of my life... and yes, of course I needed time to heal, process, grieve and just be. However, I could have also battled what happened, staying in a level of denial and finding blame somewhere for what seemed such an unfair set of circumstances.

The grief I healed wasn't done by waving a magic wand. In fact, during my major transformational journey – the part where the caterpillar closes itself into a cocoon before spreading its wings and taking flight as butterfly – I also went through a divorce. This person had been a best friend for years and a soulmate, the same person who fathered the son that passed away.

With Endings Come Beginnings

Why am I sharing this most tragic part of my life with you? I summed up several years of my life to give you an overview of the depth of hurt, grief, and suffering I went through. I did this to show you that it's possible to come out the other end, not as a wounded person carrying unresolved baggage, but as a resilient, thriving, massively transformed person, woman, and now mother. I did end up, many years later, surviving near death from a mis-diagnosed tumor, and also have the experience of a most precious, amazing gift come to me. I gave birth to an amazing, wonderful girl.

Do we have to suffer in order to reap the benefits of wisdom and life's rewards? No, not necessarily, but pain and suffering are, without a doubt a common occurrence in this life. The degree to which we experience and handle them depends on our perceptions.

Power Tool for Transformation

If you can get a basic, simple understanding of how your mind works, you will be a cut above in advancing against your block or issue. There are millions of books and courses on the power of your mind. To save you 20 years of research and studying, it comes down to the fact that your mind simply tries to protect you from perceived pain... and what you tell it, say aloud, and think plays a big role.

While positive affirmations are the tip of the iceberg, they are an important part of that iceberg. Your mind believes what you tell it and if you're thinking, saying, and doing things that are out of alignment, it causes your brain to short-circuit and miss the target.

For example, let's say you've been wanting to advance in your career but you're constantly sabotaging this by showing up late to work. Every time your boss asks to speak with you, you say the opposite of what you want. Hence, your actions (showing up to work late), your words, and your thoughts are not aligning.

Let's take it a step further and say that on your way to work, you are stressed thinking about how horrible the commute is. It may actually be horrible with lots of traffic. You have few options, but in the very given moment you can choose to sing, laugh, and not have negative and horrible thoughts about it. This counteracts the negativity immediately and sets you on your way to changing your reality... all by changing your thoughts.

Thoughts + Words + Actions

The mind also doesn't really care or know what's actually "real." If you imagine biting into a lemon, your body reacts as if you actually just bit into a lemon. Elite athletes are trained in these visualization techniques to improve their game and skills. They literally imagine going through the motion of whatever they need to do to advance in their skill for their particular sport. The body reacts to this "imagined" thinking and they are well on their way to first place by causing neurophysiological changes in their mind/body connection... and now so are you. Hurray!

The next step for you to go deeper and further, especially if you've had some long-time issues preventing you from getting past big hurdles, is to use mind/body techniques. With a session from a professional, using techniques such as hypnosis, NLP, and other state-of-the-art transformational techniques, you can cut through years of talk therapy and self-analysis and get right to the root of your issues. This transforms them easily and permanently out of your life, making way for bigger, better accomplishments in your personal and professional success. The key is getting to the root.

Hypnosis has been used for hundreds of years, and is backed by research as a proven method for clearing depression, anxiety, and PTSD (Post Traumatic Stress Disorder), as well as addictions, weight loss, and creating confidence. Some people get a little uneasy about that word "hypnosis," so I'm going to bust a myth for you right now. Yes, it's important to work with a trusted professional, but hypnosis is simply being in a super relaxed state of mind. It's nothing to be afraid of at all. Hypnotherapy is far different than stage hypnosis where a comedian/hypnotist gets people to squawk like a chicken on stage. If hypnotists actually had unconscious control over you, then they would be billionaires because they'd simply trick their clients into handing over all their money. I'm joking to prove a point. When you are in a relaxed state of mind, you are still in complete control. You simply have access to even more parts of your whole being... and you can easily shift out of patterns which have not been serving you.

Coaches, experts, and entrepreneurs often deal with issues surrounding abundance. This issue can even crop up despite the coach, expert, or entrepreneur being somewhat successful in business. A subconscious belief is running in the background saying, "I'm not worthy of lots of money," despite your attempt to gain financial freedom.

For others, you may find yourself getting into the same bad relationships over and over. You read books, talk to therapists, but no matter what, you find yourself repeating those not so healthy relationships. The subconscious program could be running in there – something your mind picked up along the way in life, most likely when you were young – and now your *conscious* wishes, hopes, dreams, and goals are in direct conflict with your *subconscious* beliefs. This is where the pros come in. With advanced hypnotherapy, in as little as one session (sometimes up to three), you can completely heal and permanently transform years of blocks that would take half a lifetime to otherwise clear.

Bonus

The first step to permanent, powerful change is creating a new habit, giving you access to your own limitless magnificence. Any issues you struggle with came about as repetitive thoughts and actions, whether you were consciously aware of them or not. Some took a lifetime to become current problems and now you want them gone. Good news! It doesn't take a lifetime to reverse them.

I love giving gifts, and my free gift to you today is a completely free recording called "Ultimate Relaxation." You will literally get the benefits of total relaxation in as little as 20 to 25 minutes. Sleep deeper, have more inner peace, allow your body, mind, and soul to experience what it's like to be so calm and at peace that your life begins to feel like a vacation.

Why relaxation? Ultimate relaxation is the state you need to be in more often in order to manifest your dreams and clear out the clutter that's preventing you from ultimate success.

To download your bonus gift recording for Ultimate Relaxation please visit www.TheParentingParadise.com and within minutes you'll be loving life and riding your highway to success (without the traffic jam).

And parents, I've got an extra bonus for you! ... my top tool for taming tantrums to household harmony!

JENNIFER CARMAN

JENNIFER CARMAN, the Pineapple Parenting Coach, is the founder of The Parenting Paradise. Her expertise in the mind/body wellness field as an advanced hypnotherapist, coupled with her love for children, allows her to give parents the tools they need to transform their toughest struggles. As a positive parenting educator, and mom, with years of training and experience, along with her unique intuitive gifts and compassion, she transforms the homes of families with toddlers to teens from chaos into harmony. She lovingly provides parents the ability to create relationships with their children and maintain calm and compassionate parenting.

She has professional clients worldwide and has two published books as well as a children's audio book.

Why the Pineapple Parenting Coach? Because sometimes parenting can feel about as good as hugging a pineapple. Ouch!... But we know there's a yummy, sweet fruit inside, and we just need to find out how to get to it and enjoy it. Jennifer shows you how and gives you tools you can use throughout your childrearing journey.

SECRETS OF STANDING OUT
IN A CROWDED WORLD

JON TOY

I'LL ADMIT IT. I love Disney World.

My family growing up visited this magical place about every other year. I was fortunate enough to find my magical princess (my beautiful wife) who also happened to love Disney World. So needless to say, our pocketbooks are doomed for life! But our children have already created magical memories and will experience many more to come.

There must be something truly magical about Disney since the strange truth is that my wife and I generally hate crowded places. It's torturous for us. We are both firstborns, so when you combine large crowds with control freaks, it can be a mess!

So how do we handle a place like Disney World? Even being strategic on when we go, there is one thing that you can guarantee at Disney World – crowds of people. If you have ever visited The Magic Kingdom, you know there is a particularly grueling crowd on Main Street USA at closing. Thousands of people stream out the exit as soon as the last firework explodes in the sky. It's like a herd of cows charging the barn at supper time (I live in the beautiful farmland of Pennsylvania). Sometimes the people in the crowds even act like animals. It's a crowd. And I don't like it.

So why do I expose myself to something I despise so much? It all comes down to the fact that the enjoyment and fun far outweigh the pain. When it comes to Disney crowds, I don't need to stand out and be noticed – by anyone other than my family. Of course it helps that I'm 6'6" and have red hair. I'm hard to miss.

But in business, no matter how hard we try, we are always in a crowded place. It's not shoulder to shoulder like the mass exodus from Disney World, but you have competitors, and their constant advertisements attacking you from all directions, crowding email inboxes and demanding attention.

For brick and mortar business owners, it's a constant attack from new competition and innovations. Your employees may be looking for greener grass somewhere else. And it's a constant fighting to stay on top and be noticed by the right customers.

For a solopreneur it's the constant changing of technology, competitors copy-catting your tactics, and customers who are wishy washy and don't seem to want to do the work you're teaching them to do.

And for a rising star employee seeking to improve their career, it's the red tape of corporations, cut-throat co-workers, and the constant change and unpredictability of the economy.

It's a crowded world no matter what your profession or where your desire to succeed takes you.

You probably don't like crowds either. So what are the secrets to standing out in a crowd wherever you are in business?

Your Shirt is Bright (Visually Stand Out)

My primary business is running a sign company. I constantly notice failed attempts for businesses to stand out through signs, trade show displays, and even literature and websites.

A strategy often used by families in Disney World to ensure there are no lost souls is to buy matching shirts. The problem with this strategy is that if your shirt is white, black, or blue, it still blends into the crowd... even if your group is walking together. It might narrow your focus a bit when searching for someone, but it doesn't stand out.

You want a bright shirt. If you're going to go to the trouble of creating visual media, make them bright! Grab attention from your group and others, because they just can't miss a bright message.

Use these three easy-to-implement ideas to help your business cards and websites, banners and trade show displays, and signs at your place of business grab attention.

1. The Eyeball Test

The first thing I do to gauge the effectiveness of any visual product is the eyeball test. It's simple. Pull up on your computer monitor, or prop up a full-sized paper proof, then move back 10-20 feet so you have to squint to see it.

What stands out? Is that what you wanted your audience to see? Can it be seen clearly? Do they know what to do?

This might sound quite obvious, but many times this simple test is what the pros use first to make powerful recommendations for improvement. It may have looked great on your computer monitor, but step back for a second and see how it really looks.

If it's a website, do the same thing. Back up and see what truly grabs your attention and be sure it's what you really want clients to see and do. Your customers are smart, but probably won't use as much common sense as you might think when it comes to doing what you want them to do.

So make it easy. Pass the eyeball test first.

2. Green and Red Means Christmas

Colors are a very powerful tool in visual products. So powerful that the wrong use of color can often confuse the audience or even send the wrong message.

Green and red is a combination often saved for Christmas. Why? Because it looks like a Christmas tree and ornaments. The same thing holds true for orange and black referring to Halloween (or Amazon Prime and prisoners).

Food industries tend to lean toward red, yellow, and white (think McDonalds, Wendy's, and KFC). Studies show that these colors influence their buyers more. I don't know if it influences my buying, but if I see your visual products and they are red and yellow, I might start thinking about McDonalds.

So what do your colors and color combinations say about you? Be sure you consider this and put the right emphasis on the right color for where you want your audience's eyes and mind to focus. Avoid distractions of too many colors, or colors that compete for their attention as they view your information.

You want to get them to the next step – whatever that is – so make that where they naturally focus their attention and do it using the right colors.

3. K.I.S.S. (Keep it simple stupid)

You're not stupid. And your customers aren't either. But many times in life we make things far too complex. So we need to keep it simple.

If you are using a visual tool to guide or direct your customers toward something, it needs to be simple.

Physical signs aren't brochures. Billboards only get 1.5 seconds to read and see. Even long copy websites and letters need to guide the reader on a journey that can't be complex. We must keep it simple.

Don't use unnecessary words or explanations. Tell stories in simple terms. Talk to your reader as if you are having a conversation, not proving the theory of relativity.

People are people. Keep it simple.

Visual solutions are needed in almost every business. Take a look at what you're using for your website, your brochures, your book, your physical sign needs, live event posters and banners, trade show displays and more. If you can pass these three simple tests – the eyeball test, the color test, and keeping it simple – you are well on your way to success and to standing out in a crowd!

I Just Need More...

Standing out in a crowded world of business takes effort and strategy. From securing more leads and customers, to advancing your career or trying to be the industry leader, the same basic fundamentals hold true.

Arguably the best coach of all time – Vince Lombardi – was known for starting out the first practice of the season by holding up a football and announcing, "Gentlemen, this is a football!" He started with the basics to remind his team that they could accomplish their goals by going back to basics to achieve maximum success.

These three basic ideas will help you stand out in a crowd no matter what your end goal may be.

Hello... Is Anybody There?

Your first step is to just show up... and show up well.

When I first started my business I was constantly told that so much of success is just showing up. I wasn't sure I fully understood what that meant but now I see how true it is. So often the crowd doesn't even show up. So you must show up.

Show up on time. Show up when not expected. Show up prepared. Show up and show up well. How you define "well" depends on what crowd you're trying to stand out in, but show up and show up well!

How can you wow the person you're meeting with next? What unexpected thing might you introduce to the conversation? Looks matter, so what look are you trying to showcase to the person you are meeting or speaking with – or that is finding you for the first time through internet or other media?

Show up... and show up well!

I'll scratch your back if you scratch mine? What??

Any crowd is consistent in one thing – lots of unknowns all gathering together. The best way to avoid a crowd, or to stand out and shine, is to become known. The best way to become known is to seek and build real relationships. The more genuine you are and the more real you are, the stronger the relationship will become.

As a man of faith, I'm drawn to a verse in the Bible – Philippians 2:5 – that guides me to have the same attitude as Jesus Christ in all my relationships. It then goes on to describe that attitude which boils down to putting others first.

Even if you don't have the same faith I do, it's easy to see that our world does not promote putting others first. But many times we view putting others first as having to cower to them or let them walk all over us. That's not the truth.

We live in a world where everything seems to come with a catch. *You scratch my back I'll scratch yours. What's in it for me?* When we value others above ourselves we are seeking to build real relationships.

So we should listen more than we talk. Seek to understand before being understood. Value others' opinions and have conversations with respect and dignity – even if we are worlds apart in agreement.

If you want to stand out in your crowd, then listen more, control your emotions, and work diligently to help other people feel important and accomplished. In the end, this helps you accomplish far more than you thought possible and you'll stand out in the crowd.

"You will get all you want in life,
if you help enough other people get what they want."

– Zig Ziglar

Step Up to the Microphone

My secondary business is coaching entrepreneurs and business owners on ways to improve their business through marketing automation, customer relationships, and sales strategies.

Remember: You are the expert! Whatever you are talking to someone about in your field, you are the authority. For some reason it's hard for us to grasp this simple fact and claim it.

For years in the sign industry there have been customers telling us "You're the expert. I trust you." Even with that constant affirmation, we struggle with stating factually that we are the experts.

You have a microphone for your expertise. Your platform is right in front of you – whatever that may be. So step up to the microphone and express yourself.

Unfortunately in today's social media world, platforms get abused and opinions become gold-standard facts in many consumers' eyes. But when it comes to you and your knowledge and expertise, become the expert.

Speak confidently about your solutions. Explain them with expertise and understanding. Refer back to the point above about building relationships, but express your expertise. It's okay to be the expert and not have your solution chosen. It doesn't change the fact that you are still the expert. You must be confident of this.

Do you use your platform to present your solution?

Are you confident in your solutions even if not selected?

Do you find ways to get your message out to others so they know you are the expert?

How are you communicating with those who need your expertise right now?

Step right up to the microphone. Your audience is waiting.

Can You See Me Now?

The Verizon commercial a few years ago had an actor constantly asking, "Can you hear me now?" My question for your audience is, "Can they see you now?"

Whether it's a visual solution you improve upon, or a better ability to build relationships – they can see you and they will notice you in a crowd!

So pick one of the strategies presented above and stand out in your crowd today!

JON TOY

JON TOY knows how to get things done. You won't ever hear him say, "There isn't enough time." He owns a seven-figure brick and mortar sign franchise, coaches small business owners through one-on-one and group mastermind meetings, is an entertaining speaker, and the author of two books.

His most recent *Geared For Growth* takes you on a journey through the eyes of a small business owner looking to grow.

Jon's unique *5 Gears System* helps you turn your business into one that can run with or without you, and lets you focus on what you like to do!

When not growing his businesses he is always with his family or serving with his church family and appreciating the blessings of life.

Taking Pride in Building the Body You Love: Simply and Without Feeling Overwhelmed

Lola White

AS I SIT AND WRITE, I am ten weeks pregnant and feel I am starting the mommy cycle all over again...

Something about this moment is nostalgic, like I have been here before. There are so many reflections happening, almost an unveiling of truths. I am experiencing a blend of excitement, fear, and unease, but yet under it all there is *love*.

The number one quality that is stronger than any overwhelming feeling that hijacks our once positive thoughts is love. In this moment, what I find to love is the fact that this is a gift many wish they could have, and for that I am grateful.

I know what it is like to lose something you love – especially a child – and what it can do to the body and emotions. My daughter is our beautiful *rainbow baby*. She means the world to us and to all who know her. I strive to teach her that the ultimate quality to have is *love,* and if you lead with that you will be able to overcome many obstacles.

I wasn't always this way: positive, outgoing, energetic, upbeat, or even social. In fact, I was quite the opposite and opposed to having any type of family life. I allowed my past to scar me. It led me to believe I was broken and damaged and had little to offer. I told myself lies, frequently ones that said I could never change, that fate was controlling my future. Nothing ever changed and when it did it was for the worse, not the better.

This one thought and moment of clarity all came from someone telling me – and showing me – "*You* can give better, you have limitless potential, and I believe in you! *Do you?*"

I had previously been asking myself: "What if things could be different?" Once I removed the need to know whether things could work out, I realized I had been blocking myself from receiving a better life. Then I learned to ask: "What if reality could be as crazy and limitless as I dream? What if I am the only one standing in my way... regardless of past, present, future, or background?"

I had been hiding so long I am not sure I knew any other way. Despite trying to change, I exposed my deepest desire to become more. In my heart, I knew I couldn't go it alone. For the first time I started to listen to that heart, and it woke me up to truths – and also to misconstrued lies – that had gotten lost over time.

Is there anyone in your life who has made you feel this way? Someone who finally saw you for you? That someone opened my eyes and it was almost like there was no going back. There was no more lying to myself, no more excuses.

Life has a funny way of throwing you exactly what you swore you would never do, then allowing you the opportunity to master it. A colleague once said: "Your greatest trials become your greatest treasures." I realized I could use what I had been feeling to fuel my ambition for a greater cause. The cause was larger than me.

I discovered my passion was to show up for a generation of women who believe they are broken. This goal lit me up. I remember smiling from ear to ear. I could feel the sense of ease come over me. I could see the vision before the journey even began.

I come from a very, very long line of strong women who have given everything for their family, friends, and others, but there was still a void when it came to their own value and self-worth. It is amazing and comforting to see these women give everything they have, but it's also heart breaking to see them emotionally and mentally drained... and physically in poor health.

Our personal health and wellness affects how we show up in our world. When we take care of ourselves, it positively affects how we are able to contribute in our day to day lives. Supporting ourselves and, for once, putting ourselves as women first, is actually an unselfish act.

The truth is, the level of our health impacts not only our own success in life, but also our family's health, and the health of our business.

You have two choices. You can *try*, or you can actually *do*.

In that moment, I saw my future filled with optimism and hope. It unfolded by stopping the stories I had told myself about how ugly I was, how fat I was, how dysfunctional my life had been, and how much time I had wasted and how nothing would ever change. If you believe these lies, then it turns out you will be right. Because believing the lies gives them truth. Instead, why not give birth to opportunity and trust that sparks confidence? Take back control of your health. It will take time, but over that same time your reality will change.

There are many paths to take on a hike, and even more so in life. That doesn't mean only one path is going to be suitable for everyone. My journey was my own, and with trial and error I discovered over the course of eight years what worked and didn't work. Now 12 years later, I discover I am still navigating that journey and excited to do so.

You must understand that your body is always changing. Success comes in life and health by being adaptable to what is needed in any given moment. Sometimes all that is needed is to just be present. We are human beings, not human doings.

This diet or that diet, this workout or that workout... we should not forget or become distracted about what remains most important... and for everyone that is different. For me, I just wanted to be happy, feel better in my skin, and increase my energy and confidence. I wanted to trust again... to trust that I could make good decisions for myself. I wanted to trust in my body's ability to recover. I wanted to create impact and be that example.

I wanted so many things. I desired for my reality to change because I believed it was possible. And now I know it is possible for everyone.

The risk or sacrifice you perceive has to be worth the reward. How can you benefit by making these adjustments? It is a very powerful thought because for me it allowed me to go deeper than just the superficial wants. It led me to discover my motivating factors that would outlast the temporary and short-lived excitement.

I started to see that all the events that took place were just momentary. Although they left deep impressions, they were just events for which I chose to hold on to the emotion, denying anything was wrong, telling myself that I was fine where I was.

In fact I tried to hide by padding myself with an excess fifty pounds and poor health conditions. I always felt pain and discomfort.

We have all heard the phrase "Go big or go home," whether it is in relation to business or personal life. Taking a risk or making an enormous sacrifice can lead to positive outcomes, but if you are a busy mama and wife, you must avoid the belief that sacrificing your health is okay.

You can call it the guilt, shame, blame, or mom-card. I am not your typical have-it-together organized mama who wakes up 5:30 a.m. to attend yoga and drink my green smoothie in time to pack school lunches and have breakfast made, then post online about how perfect my life is. Frankly, I like a little more chaos in my life.

What I am here to make you aware of is that with all the motivation, inspiration, and resources out there, it's still okay to feel like the game of life is failing you. It's okay to stop and wonder where that 20 pounds of stored body-fat came from. But it's not okay to talk to yourself as if you are your own worst enemy.

But first you must become aware of the self-talk. If you were not aware, you would not care. I realized that my awareness and dissatisfaction with my energy levels and progress in business and in life was because I knew I deserved better, but what was missing was how to bridge the gap and connect the dots from my health to the quality with which I could show up for my business and my family.

If you want to get better at this game of life, there needs to be a plan with consistent routines to brave the hectic moments and keep everything in place. You schedule the dog's vet visits, routine dental care, a tune-up for the car, and you even schedule when to pay your bills. Hopefully there's a schedule for when the kids need to take a shower and be in bed... but where is the time for you? You do so much for others as a powerful creative being. Maybe every other month you actually manage to get your nails done, but is that enough to keep you sane? You tell me.

The game of life is about enhancing the moments that matter, and one way of doing that is by supporting your mental, emotional, and physical well being – and that also goes for your sexual well being. This is a true balance of health.

When we optimize these moments that matter, we allow ourselves to be truly present and without the need or feeling we must or "should" be somewhere else. The truth is that we are not somewhere else. We are right where we are and if we can see that arguing with reality only creates frustration and confusion, we will soon desire to keep our minds and body present.

Planning and having a consistent routine will allow us to make time for what is needed, but also create boundaries that are necessary. It may sound robotic in the beginning but once you get consistent, it becomes a no-brainer to select your "yes's" and your "no's." The game of life is balancing your time and energy by scaling your health and fitness. Motivation is a very small part to success; it is the desire to fight for what it is you believe you deserve, and when you believe it, there is nothing that can stand in your way. This is why you must never underestimate powerful resources and tools you have to bridge the gap to building the body you love.

Will-power is short lived. There is an incredible intensity and exhilaration that comes from motivation and feeling inspired to start something; it can be just the tool needed to get us going. Creating the desire to do something lights a fire within ourselves... but what happens a few days or even weeks later when that fire or motivation begins to wane? We can start to question ourselves, creating doubt, comparisons, obstacles, and even the belief that "I can't do this!"

This is often what happens for every resolution to get fit and healthy when starting a new diet, or maybe it's the post-baby weight we are looking to lose after five years. It's just baby fat, right?

Motivation gets us hyped, but then we are reminded of our past failures. This is why motivation is not enough. It is not enough to combat our daily stresses or the reality of the negative self-talk we do on a minute-by-minute basis. We wake up, breathe, and the first thing we think of is how much there is to do, and that there is no way we will have enough time. Then we look in the mirror at our gorgeous blessed body and see cellulite ripples and a muffin-top post C-section. We forget about having those three beautiful kids. Instead we complain to ourselves that everything is wrong.

It is impossible to rise above this kind of self-talk and find the will-power and motivation to continue unless you are reminding your body of your own worth. Give back to the beautiful vibrant soul that you are, without making apology for the time that is given.

Gratitude is grace and presence. Think of your most expansive moment when you felt your heart open and wide and enamored by the tiny details of perhaps a nature scene, or maybe witnessing your child's first bicycle ride. Remind yourself how beautiful life is and forever remember the grace and gratitude you felt in those moments. You weren't trying to be anywhere else.

We don't often think of gratitude as being part of our health but when we are in a gracious state of mind, the body stops fighting itself. It is at peace and ease and can recover.

Clients often tell me they lose weight on vacation, even while eating what they want. Go figure! Stress is a major reason why the body was blocked from losing weight. Stress drains the body of energy, and our ability to be present in the moment is thwarted because we are always worried about what is going to go wrong.

Worrying is like a rocking chair that gets us nowhere.

Planning and being prepared is very different. This sets the body up for success and will allow you to focus on the theme of building the body you love.

As I dream beautiful dreams for the new child to come in my life, I know I must now take care of myself as well. The excitement, fear, and unease are still humming in the background, yet still... underneath it all... is love. Through grace and gratitude, we can all find enough strength to love ourselves more completely, to stop the negative self-talk, and instead learn to fall in love again. This time with our own selves and our bodies.

When we give the body what it needs, it will heal.

LOLA WHITE

LAUREN (LOLA) WHITE, N.T.P., is a Nutritional Therapist, Gut Health Specialist, and an advocate for busy moms looking to balance it all while remaining healthy and strong... without losing their cool!

Her wake-up call was high blood pressure, a kidney mass, and being told she was clinically obese. She made the connection between the way food was impacting her decisions with the beliefs that she should just settle for what was and always had been.

By changing her relationship with food and starting to nourish her body, the excess weight fell off, inches were reduced, and a confident and clear woman emerged... one who is now on a mission to help other women who face the same struggles.

She enjoys hiking, weight lifting, helping others, traveling the world, and most of all being present with her family. Lola will soon welcome a second daughter into the world!

Learn how losing the weight can be a liberating side effect for building the body you love. Download your *"Free Guide to Understanding Your Cravings"* at:

whiteiristc.com

AN OBSTRUCTION

MAGDA CASTAÑEDA

"SHE HAS AN OBSTRUCTION," my brother said over the phone. He had taken my mom to the hospital because her eyes were very yellow. I couldn't help but cry. As a nurse, I knew that wasn't a good sign. I took a deep breath and managed to tell him, "It's okay. She'll be okay. I'll be there as soon as I can."

Mami and most of the women in my family (on my Mom's side), had been diagnosed with diabetes at a young age – maybe in their early 30s. At the time I was very young, and decided I didn't want to join the club. Somehow I wanted to break the chain. I was always conscious about it, but after giving birth to three kids and as I aged, I noticed how my weight had built up on me.

Losing Mami to pancreatic cancer was the most difficult thing I have ever witnessed because I was looking at it through a child's lens as well as a nurse's. Mami was also a nurse and her specialty was hospice care. She was certainly conscious of everything that was happening to her until the last minute.

When I lost Mami, I felt a huge shift inside me. I had to rediscover the world without her. I was her only female child and she had been like a second mom to my children. It was then when I started my quest, which I called: "In the pursuit of health."

Many things followed Mami's death, including the death of my cousin Brenda, who was only one year older than me. She called on Black Friday 2013 and said, "I've lost more than 15 pounds because I keep vomiting everything I eat, and I'm in pain. Do you think I should go to the hospital?" She was concerned because she didn't have health insurance.

"I think you should go right now! Please don't wait," I told her.

She ended up going to the hospital two days later. When I called to check on her, she answered, "They say I have an obstruction."

I couldn't believe my ears. "Who said that and what kind of obstruction?"

"The doctor told me I may have an obstruction in my duodenum," she replied.

That's the part of the intestines that usually obstructs first when there's a tumor in the head of the pancreas. I couldn't believe it! "I'll be there tomorrow," I told her.

When I walked into her hospital room she looked happy to see me and nervous at the same time. The nurse had told her the doctor was coming to speak with her. "I'm so glad you're here," she said and we hugged and cried. Then we started laughing about memories of our childhood.

When the doctor finally walked in, he asked, "Can I talk in front of her?"

"I want her to know everything," Brenda replied.

"We think you could have a tumor on the head of your pancreas. We'll do some more testing but that's what it looks like right now. I'll schedule you for a couple of studies to be done tomorrow."

Oh boy. I couldn't believe this was happening again.

When the doctor left, Brenda said to me, "Can you imagine me being the first from our generation to die?"

"Stop the nonsense," I replied. "Don't say that."

Five months after being diagnosed, my dear cousin Brenda passed due to pancreatic cancer.

That was two in a row in about a year and a half. During research of my family's health history I also found that my grandmother's sister had died due to pancreatic cancer. Now, I was getting really scared.

I didn't just need to avoid diabetes, but also pancreatic cancer as well.

And it was becoming harder and harder not to be overweight. My energy was dropping and I felt fatigued, frustrated, and with very little hope.

At five feet tall I was up to 160 pounds. I knew I really had to do something if I wanted to reach my goal of not being diagnosed with diabetes. I was already pre-diabetic at 46 years old and I desperately needed a way out.

I had seen what diabetes could do, not only with the experience in my family but also through my renal failure patients. Most of my nursing experience is as a Certified Nephrology Nurse. I actually teach technicians and nurses how to take care of renal failure patients. I own a training center and I talk about this every day.

I knew I needed to do something and I felt like I was running out of time.

Every new year feels like a new opportunity for me and that's when I choose to make things different – especially, since it's Mami's death anniversary. She passed on the morning of January 2nd. So like many other people, I promised myself that I would be consistent and follow through with my health goals. Despite great intentions, I would fall off the bandwagon even before the end of the month. But this year was different. I started training as an Integrative Nutrition Health Coach and although I had been a nurse for 23 years, this new training brought a different perspective – another way of looking at things. Very different than what I was used to.

For the first time in my life, I wasn't thinking about what type of med could help. I started to go deeper. I started to understand that the root cause of many of our conditions and weight gain is not age or genetics. It's our food choices.

I started to defy what my primary care doctor was telling me and move in another direction. This is not what I recommend you should do, but it was definitely what I did.

Learning more and more, the word "sugar" kept coming up. It all started to make sense. I decided to cut down on my sugar intake, limiting it to 50g or less, with 25g of those coming from fruits. I counted my sugar and eliminated everything that had "high fructose corn syrup" or "fructose" written on the label.

The first three days were the most intense. I felt headaches, my energy was low and I had a few episodes of craving attacks. But I didn't give in. Because I was expecting this to happen, I had planned my days to have less things to do. I added a one-hour nap into my schedule and made sure I was eating nuts and seeds – raw almonds, cashews, and sunflower seeds. At the time, I was still drinking one cup of coffee in the morning. I made sure I had it first thing after my meditation. Just black coffee with cinnamon. I also increased my water intake. This gave me a sense of refreshment. I felt lighter and even cleaner inside. I also saw my skin change and I felt less bloated each day.

It started working. I could see the pounds melt away. First it was five, then 15. Soon I had lost 20 and altogether I lost 34 pounds in a period of six months. All because I started to count sugar.

Anyone can count sugar! Doing this has not just helped me lose weight, but also to have sustained energy during the day, and feel alive, powerful, and beautiful. The cravings are gone and I enjoy creating new recipes that are delicious and low in sugar. Counting my macros and planning my meals for the week is exciting to me. I don't have to guess what I'll be eating, nor do I have to eat out because I didn't plan my food. Now, it's part of my routine and it feels so satisfying when I accomplish it every week.

Cutting sugar is tough but doable. Sugar withdrawal symptoms will last about three days – headaches, fatigue, weakness. The body must get used to burning fat instead of sugar for energy. But when you crave something sweet and you actually eat it, usually it's in the form of a simple carbohydrate or refined sugar. This makes the body absorb the sugar quickly and send it to your bloodstream, activating the insulin response. When insulin comes, it's like sweeping the trash under the rug. It pushes the sugar out of the bloodstream and into the cells until they are full and nothing else will fit. When the cells don't accept more sugar brought by insulin, this is called "insulin resistance." This sugar is brought to the liver but the liver can't process all of it. So in exchange, it creates fat. Many people with insulin resistance also have fatty liver. From there the fat is pushed back into the bloodstream, increasing cholesterol and triglycerides. In addition, the same fat starts to surround your waistline. This is visceral fat, which is the most dangerous. It puts you at risk for high cholesterol and triglycerides, making your chances of heart disease even greater. This is without counting the risk of pre-diabetes and diabetes. When you continue to eat a high-sugar diet, this becomes a vicious circle.

Counting my macros, planning, and cooking my own meals have been part of my success in this journey. I'm able to conrol the ingredients and measure my food. What doesn't get measured, can't be controlled.

A Method to the Madness

I recommend eating inside a 12-hour period, having three meals, counting your sugar, and not eating more than 50g (25g from fruit), drinking half of your body weight (in pounds) in ounces of water, and doing some type of daily exercise.

Here's an example of how that looks in my day:

6:00 am	Wake up
	Drink my green tea or detox bomb (12 oz)
6:30 am	Workout – 20 oz of water
8:00 am	Breakfast (1–3 hours after waking up)
	20 oz of water
	20 oz of water
1:00 pm	Lunch
	20 oz of water
6:00pm	Dinner (no less than 3 hours before bedtime)

I like to plan my meals on Sundays for what I'll eat Monday through Thursday because those are my busiest days. Fridays I work from home and cook during my Facebook Live show every week. You can find the show by searching @healthcoachmagda. It's in Spanish, but it's fun and the recipes are delicious! Saturdays and Sundays I have time to get creative in the kitchen.

For Monday through Thursday, I plan one breakfast, one lunch and four different dinners. From there I create a shopping list and either head to the grocery store or order through Instacart. (The latter is my favorite because it saves me so much time!)

I like to cook and prepare easy meals I can place in my glass containers and store in the refrigerator. This also saves a lot of time during the week.

A breakfast that helps control my sugar intake:

CocoBlue Smoothie
1 cup unsweetened coconut milk
¼ cup frozen blueberries
2 tbsp chia seeds
1 cup baby spinach
2 tbsp almond butter
3 tbsp unsweetened Greek yogurt

Makes about 16 oz when blended. Use as a meal replacement. It has everything you need, with *only 4.4g of sugar.*

For lunch I can have a jar salad. They are delicious. You really have to try this one. I use a wide mouth glass mason jar. The idea is to add all the wet ingredients at the bottom and the dry ones on the top, then you can seal and even eat from the jar.

Jar Salad

2 tbsp no-sugar dressing
   I create my own:
   2 tbsp red wine vinegar
   2 tbsp Dijon mustard
   ¼ tsp salt
   pepper to taste
   ⅓ olive oil
½ cup cooked sliced carrots
½ medium tomato cut in wedges
½ medium onion into slices
¼ cup cooked quinoa
4 oz boneless, skinless chicken breast cut into cubes
¼ cup part-skim low-sodium shredded mozzarella
1 cup baby spinach

Stack ingredients inside the mason jar in this order. I usually make four and store in the refrigerator. Because the cover is air-tight, they can last all week long. *Only 8.4g of sugar.*

I choose different meals for my dinner, but here is one I especially enjoy.

Steak (or Salmon) with Zucchini & Summer Squash

Place a sheet of parchment paper on a sheet pan.
On one side, place about 4 pieces of round thin-cut steak.
On the other, place:

> 1 zucchini cut into slices
> 1 summer squash cut into slices
> ½ red pepper
> ½ green pepper cut into slices
> ½ red onion cut into slices

Season with salt, pepper, onion powder, garlic salt, oregano and turmeric, then sprinkle with 1 tbsp olive oil. Place sheet pan in oven and bake 20 minutes at 400 °F. *Only 11.2g of sugar.*

The sugar content between these three meals is 24g. Since I've mastered the method, I now average only 25-30g of sugar daily. I don't even reach the 50g.

Knowing how to count your sugar intake is important because it can add up fast. Many people eat Activia yogurt for breakfast. The label says it has probiotics and it's low-fat. Commercials make us believe it's great for our gut health because of the live culture contents. But let's look closer – really read the nutrition facts, not only the front label.

In a 4 oz. Dannon Activia vanilla low-fat yogurt, the front label promotes: probiotic yogurt, low-fat yogurt, natural flavors, calcium and vitamin D for strong bones, live and active probiotics, live cultures, and gluten-free. All this is on the front label. With all this information there's no need to read the back. Right? Wrong!

Let's now look at the nutrition facts. First, notice the serving size. The container is 4 oz. and that's the serving size, but other products like commercial fruit juices have two or sometimes more servings per bottle. Remember that nutrition facts are based on a single serving size – not the entire bottle. Moving down the nutrition label, you will usually find the total fat, cholesterol, sodium, carbohydrates, fiber, sugar, and protein. All are important, but for the sake of your time let's concentrate on sugar.

The sugar amount in one serving of this yogurt is 13g – in just 4 oz.! Plus, it does not state any fiber content. Fiber would help your body absorb sugars slower so the insulin response would not trigger abruptly.

What does this mean? Eating this 4 oz. vanilla yogurt will not make you full. Sugar will be absorbed quickly and will also feed the bad bacteria in your gut instead of the good ones.

So it really defeats the purpose of eating it for gut health. And chances are that you may not only eat one but two to feel satisfied. Plus it contains modified food starch – try to avoid anything that states "modified."

You can go through the 50g of sugar allowance that I'm recommending in a snap because you still have to eat during the rest of your day. The Diabetes Council 2017 states that the average American consumes about *126g of sugar per day*. But the body wasn't created to handle all of that sugar. Its manifestations show up in the form of visceral fat, diabetes, heart disease, inflammation, autoimmune diseases, cancer and much more.

If you would like to learn more about how you can start controlling your sugar intake, I have a special gift for you. Jumpstart your weight loss by decreasing your sugar for 14 days.

Visit https://14dayswithoutsugar.com/ to learn how you can follow a 14-day system to start losing weight and gain control of your chronic illnesses.

Just 14 days is all it takes to see results, even if you've tried many diets before. What you'll get is not a diet, but a guide to start a new sugar-free lifestyle. The best part is that it's completely free!

MAGDA CASTAÑEDA

MAGDA CASTAÑEDA is an entrepreneur based in Florida. After more than 20 years working as a Registered Nurse, she decided to build and grow her own company.

She has managed to grow two small businesses in the United States generating multiple six figures of income. Magda owns both a brick and mortar and online training business. She uses online courses to train and create an impact in the lives of over 2,000 of her students.

Meet Me at the Mailbox

Marie-Paule Sinyard

SO I AM GOING TO TELL YOU EXACTLY WHAT HAPPENED.

What happened and what I did.

This is precisely how I changed my perspective and became entirely unemployable.

My journey began in a most unlikely place. It started on the bathroom floor. I was 32 and on my way to a meeting to (hopefully) close a big account I had been working on for months.

I recall feeling a little dizzy as I got into the shower. The next thing I remember was waking up on the bathroom floor – I had completely passed out, and just to make sure there was some real drama, I was hemorrhaging.

I got up, got dressed, went to my meeting, then sat in my doctor's office. I told her something was wrong and I wasn't leaving until we figured out what.

That was the day I landed the biggest account of my career.

And that was the day I found out I had Stage 4 cancer.

When the Casseroles Quit Coming – Just Walk to the Mailbox

Fast forward eight months. I was sitting in my living room staring at $250k in medical bills. My formerly lucrative financial career was now in shambles. I was still in treatment and couldn't travel for work. I couldn't meet clients, which meant I couldn't make sales, which meant I wasn't making money.

I was certain I had hit rock bottom. As luck would have it – not yet. There was a knock at the door. It was my postman armed with a certified letter from the IRS. Turned out I owed $16,000 in back taxes. Oh yeah, and I was divorcing my husband.

You see, in the midst of all the trauma and soul killing, dream-shattering turmoil, I reconnected with a cute boy from high school. He was, in short, a glorious distraction. A beautiful diversion with long eyelashes and a sweetness that was so needed. I could tell him anything and everything. And then I couldn't.

Looking at the pile of bills and that weaponized certified letter, I distinctly remember having the most vivid thought. A voice with crystal clarity in my head said, *"Marie-Paule, it would have been easier if you had just died."*

I call this dark period "the time when the casseroles quit coming." It's funny how when you are in the hospital, fighting for your life, hopped up on morphine and who knows what else, completely unaware of what is going on around you except the all-knowing fear that your pain may get ahead of your meds – that this is the time when people want to visit. Send flowers. Make you casseroles. By the time you get home, you arrogantly throw away the cheesy baked cream-of-whatever-laced meals and the well-intentioned noodle disappointment. You wash the dishes, hopefully return them to their rightful owners, and then... nothing.

When the worst is over and you are left with your thoughts and your disappointments and your self-doubt, about whether you can (or even want to) start over after a huge loss... there are no flowers, no visitors, no inedible casseroles. Everyone has moved on. Except for you. And the silence is deafening.

Your pity party is officially over and it is time for you to get on with it. Problem is, you're just *now* aware enough to *start* grieving. And if you are not careful, all hell will break loose and you can find yourself questioning both your sanity and your life station as you fill your time with mindless daytime series peppered with ads for community colleges daring you to do something, anything, but just sit there and stare.

I knew that I could keep being scared and depressed or I could do something about it. And I figured instead of looking all the way down the road to the horizon, I would just walk to the mailbox. And then keep going.

What I recognized was I had a network of people who valued me.

I had counseled people before on their big home design projects – they had asked and taken my advice on remodeling their kitchens. What if I could find someone to pay me for something I had been doing for free all along?

I had an idea. The next week I held two dinner parties at my little rental house and hoped against hope that no one would notice my almond appliances and mystery material counters. I invited everyone I knew with a house that could use some remodeling. And I hosted a ribbon-cutting for my new design business called *Marie-Paule Designing Lifespaces*.

That week I got my first design client. And over the next three years I paid off every penny of my $250k medical bill.

You can and will monetize your passion, but you have got to get your head on straight first.

Through literal sweat, blood, and tears, I uncovered and live by a system that I know works and I want to share it with you. Every time I lose sight of this truth, I mess up. Every. Single. Time. I believe with my entire heart that it will help you through the blinding fright, the mind numbing self-doubt, and the dream-trashing sense of overwhelm that can grip you when you start a new business in this strange frontier of online everything and promised overnight success (guaranteed only if you have the foresight to put your garden tools in the blender while holding your cell phone and recording yourself. Don't forget to put your hand on your hip and keep your chin down.)

So meet me at the mailbox and I will tell you a little secret that I know will help you as you brave the wilds of online marketing and offline ambiguity.

Fear Means Go. Doubt Means No.

I remember in a marketing class seeing a picture of an unfortunate old woman. If I blinked or looked at the picture long enough, at least half the time the old woman morphed into a beautiful lady in an enviable hat. The bottom line was that seeing is not always believing. And as I laid there in my hospital bed, I realized that if you shift your perspective ever so slightly, what you are certain is true, actually is questionable at best.

I hope you will never know the warp speed at which you are required to make literal life and death decisions once diagnosed with a major illness. Seriously, if it wasn't so blood-curdlingly scary it would be comical. But trust me, cancer jokes are not well received by your loved ones at this time – I tried it. Not recommended. Even if it *was* bloody hilarious.

What is remarkable to me is the parallel between the epoch-making decisions required when in medical purgatory and the constant barrage of judgments demanded of you when you are starting a new business.

The short answer is to hire an expert to help you. I mean, I didn't operate on myself. The long answer is to choose the *right* person to help you. And that is where the hat-lady perspective shift comes in.

Laying in a hospital bed day after day with nothing to look forward to but ice chips and the doctor-prescribed walk around the nurses' station leaves you a lot of time to think. About life and death and all the challenges in between. Assumptions you have made, mistakes, and misunderstandings. And sometimes. A stroke of genius.

So here it is. My claim to fame, whether you recognize it or not. "Fear means go. Doubt means no." Let me explain.

My biggest cancer-inducing realization is that we have been conditioned to misinterpret fear. We confuse it with doubt.

I think if you are scared as hell about doing something, you should stop everything and do it right now. Think about every life-changing crossroad of your life. There was no meadow frolicking. There was pure unadulterated fear. Terror even.

That fear builds more and more power the older you get and the longer you listen to it... the longer you let it rule you. But what if (hear me out), what if fear means "do it immediately"? What if fear is an indication of certainty for you? What if the inclination to run like hell in the other direction just leaves the spoils and dream manifestation to the other guy who knows better? What if you are wrong, and fear is not the old woman with the unfortunate nose? What if fear is in fact a beautiful representation of promise and certainty, beauty and perfection? I mean, what if?

Here's the rub. "Doubt means no." Or not now, anyway. Not until you feel pure unadulterated, unfiltered fear. And if you do it right and often enough, you will come to welcome fear. Invite it over for wine even. But you have to learn how to distinguish between the two.

Trust me, you will get better at it as you go along, but here is a good place to start. Let's say you are getting ready to spend $2000 a month on marketing. Guaranteed to save your life, propel your business into the profitable stratosphere, and frankly do everything but your laundry over the next 365 days.

You listen to yourself. That voice inside your head. Really listen. And notice if that voice is expressing fear or doubt. Because there *is* a difference.

Fear Example: "I am scared that it is not going to work. What if I fail?" I mean, you literally just said you feel fear. If you have nothing else to go on, this would indicate that you should do it. Right. Now.

Doubt Example: "I have no idea what the heck they are talking about. I have so many questions I don't even know where to start."

Here's how to tell the difference. You cannot feel real fear if you aren't certain on some level about what you are considering. I mean, how can you be scared pantsless of something you're indifferent to? You can't. Fear is impregnated with an inherent action. An alertness. An awareness. A go position. Fear wakes you up. Fear can save your bacon. It makes you take notice of your surroundings and possible strategies to get from where you are to somewhere, anywhere else. Even if that somewhere is the elaborate form of procrastination called indecision.

Alternately, doubt doesn't unleash you or propel you in any way. It makes you hesitate. It is the love child of paralysis and trauma. It is demoralizing, demobilizing, and a constant reminder of bad experiences past. It keeps you trapped, running in place. And I ask you, what is the literal point of running in place? I mean, at least sit down and have a Dorito. If nothing else, that is mildly entertaining and unquestionably yummy.

But know. Doubt is the serial killer of dreams. Its sole mission is to keep you confused and anesthetized to the possibility that with real fear comes real change, and with real change can come real success.

Challenge your doubt. Punch it in the face. As I would expect you to do to any abuser. Because sooner or later your life will be the one you deserve.

Need more proof? More evidence that doubt is a total jerk? Its hindsight is 20/20. It never shows up after you have listened to your fear and slayed the dragon. Oh no. Doubt has moved on without as much as a "Sorry, hon" to your next dream. Your next big thing that could lead to earth-shattering success and immaculate happiness. Doubt is always two paces ahead of you. Not to put too fine of a point on it, but doubt is a bastard. Full stop.

Does that freak you out? Good. Because "fear means go" and I am officially introducing the two of you.

Too scared to get all the way from where you are now to dreams accomplished? No problem. Let's just meet down the street a bit.

This is fear. And it is here for you. Follow it, honor it, and listen to it... and it will become your best partner. Your most trusted confidante. And the closest thing to guaranteed success that you will ever get.

Now go write a check for that marketing and let's get going. I'll see you at the finish line and we will toast the death of doubt. But in a totally nice way! ☺

MARIE-PAULE SINYARD

So. You've finally decided to renovate your kitchen and now you want to know how to get your dream kitchen for pennies on the dollar. That's what MARIE-PAULE SINYARD lives to do. She has redesigned, remodeled, and renovated literally hundreds of kitchens in every style from farmhouse to mid-century modern.

Marie-Paule was truly humbled to be named a leading expert in Kitchen Design and Renovation and was literally looking around for someone to hug when she was recognized by Fox, NBC, CBS, and ABC.

She adores her clients – they include everyone from her friends around the corner to the governor's family home. But most importantly she has counseled and guided countless creative homeowners across the country and together they've proven that you can get your dream kitchen accomplished on time, on budget, and in style.

Marie-Paule cannot wait for you to have your first cocktail party in your new kitchen. She wants to hear every detail and walk with you every step of the way to get your dream kitchen accomplished.

To learn more, visit mariepaulehome.com or contact her directly at marie-paule@mariepaulehome.com

Build-A-Brand

Mimi Sheffer

The Benefits of Branding

LIFE IS FUNNY. We can have our whole lives planned out yet somehow end up in a completely different place than expected. But sometimes, that place is right where we were meant to be... and these unexpected paths gift us the greatest blessings.

Back in the 1980s, quote buttons were all the rage. TGI Friday's called them "flair" and my friends and I wore them on our jean jackets. There was something magical about those sarcastic little buttons that perfectly stated my thoughts. And so, in my teen years, I began unknowingly collecting quotes. By my sophomore year of college, I glued written quotes all over the back of my dorm door. I wish I could say they were all enlightened and wise but the only one I can remember is shallow and superficial: "MBA = BMW."

As an adult, and especially since the advent of Facebook, I've found that shared quotes have incredible power. In a tough moment, the right phrase can change a bad mood, validate one's feelings, build a sense of community, or provide a laugh or a cry. I've come to believe they hold magical power... or they wouldn't be so frequently shared.

In my own direct sales business, I found that sharing quotes helped me create a unique voice and differentiate myself. So when a friend suggested that my designs were so nice that others might want to purchase them, I realized graphics could become an effective branding tool for people in direct sales, like me. My education and career were spent in sales and marketing but I wasn't an expert on branding, so I began studying everything I could find on the subject.

Several months, and thousands of quotes later, I finally opened my online graphic quote store and Branding Masterclass.

So how does branding work, and how can it help sell online? Good question!

If you are in Direct Sales or Consultative Sales, you have a lot of competition in the social media space.

"Side-gigs" have become more mainstream, and almost everyone we know is using social media to advertise theirs. The only problem is the flood of ads in the newsfeed, and people have become increasingly numb to it.

Most direct sellers and consultative sales agents (think realtors, financial advisors, insurance salesmen) take a traditional stance on social media – pushing out information to their networks. Yet savvy shoppers reject that because it feels... well, pushy... and they scroll right past. The new psychology of posting for affect is to completely change *how* we post on social media... by instead *pulling* people to us.

There are several ways to do this. But first you have to change your perspective.

When most people think of branding, they picture a logo or slogan, but branding is so much more. Boiled down to its most basic essentials, branding is what people say about a company when describing it to someone else. It's the sum of all the parts of a product, service and... seller. To be effective in direct or consultative sales, you need to become your own brand.

Let's do a little exercise. Close your eyes and name the companies that come to mind in the first few seconds. I bet you listed giants like Nike, Apple, Coca-Cola, Google, and Starbucks. Those companies have done a really effective job of marketing and public relations because their names, logos, product images, and the company's identity stick with you long after you've been exposed to them.

Public relations factor into the formula as well. You probably wouldn't recognize a company's beneficial public relations – like what charities they support or causes they care about – but if a company responds poorly to a crisis or incident, the bad PR can have a resounding negative impact on their brand and image. So branding is the total package – it's a company's product, logo, slogan, marketing strategy, product placement, identity, description, and even its public relations.

As someone who sells or offers the same products or services as many other people, you need to have a differentiation factor. You need to give customers a reason to buy from you. To maximize your effectiveness, you need to stand out among your peers who sell the same products or services. You need to *create* your own brand and focus on building relationships on and off social media. Become a magnet, pulling people to you with your messaging and your presence.

Here is how to build a strong personal brand using what I call Magnetic Marketing:

Step 1: Brand Yourself

You are not the products you sell or the company you represent. Your Personal Brand is all the awesome things that make you who you are. The first step is to realize that you are separate from and uniquely different to anyone else... and to celebrate that fact. You do that by figuring out who you are and how you want to present yourself to the world.

Get a sheet of paper and make a list.

What's your personality? Are you funny, sarcastic, motivational, religious, supportive, silly?

What are your passions and hobbies? Who is your family? What industry are you in? How do you want to be known by your network?

You'll want to take that list and then draw triangles for each one on a clean sheet of paper. These triangles will become your content topics. They represent who you are, what you do, your personality, your passions, where you're from, and what you value. You should end this exercise with about 10–12 content topic triangles.

A couple of them will be about your industry or line of work – one directly related to what you do, and another associated field that applies to or affects your field. One triangle will be about your family, three or four will be about your passions or hobbies, one will be about your personal philosophy or mission, one about your life pillars – or what you believe in, one about your personality, and one about your life goals.

So, if you are in the health and nutrition space, your work triangles might contain information about proper nutrition and the benefits of exercise. Your family triangles will contain your kids, spouse, pets.

Your passion triangles can vary. They might include hobbies, passions, or even where you're from. These can include your love of coffee or wine, travel, the beach... whatever you enjoy, you need to include it in your content plan. The last content triangles should be about your life goals or your hopes for the future.

These triangles fit together to make up the whole of who you are and who you want to be known as in your life. The awesome fact is you get to choose what topics to feature on your social media, but you must be authentically you. You can't lie about who you really are because people will see right through attempts to do that.

All the content on your social media feeds should fit into one of these pre-planned topics. As a business person using social media to grow your client base, it's a good rule of thumb to think of social media like a cocktail party. Avoid the "Big 3" party topics – sex, religion and politics – however, if politics is a major passion, you'll be unlikely to avoid that topic completely. Just realize that every bit of information you put out on social media goes into the mix that becomes your brand. It's a piece of information that people will use to figure out who you really are, so posting about the taboo topics will certainly alienate part of your audience.

Step 2: Create an Identity

If you're in business, you need a logo and a branding package. Don't worry. Those may sound much more serious and complicated than they really are. What you need is to decide on a color scheme, and create or buy a logo for yourself. You increase your credibility and your effectiveness by tenfold when you have your own logo and brand identity. You can go to Upwork.com or Fiverr.com and work with a designer to create a logo for about $50, or you can purchase a created logo on Etsy.com. If you want to create your own logo, try using Canva.com. It's a powerful design tool and makes designing a logo relatively easy. To create an eye-catching logo, use your name and some sort of symbol in your logo. Incorporate 2–3 colors that complement each other and that appeal to you. Experiment with fonts and colors in your first and last name and symbol. Export the logo from Canva and you're ready to go! To stay cohesive, be sure to use this logo and colors on every piece of marketing material that you create.

Step 3: Use Your Voice

Always create authentic content. It's okay to use other people's content as a guide but copied content doesn't feel authentic to your network and they'll skip past it. If you're using someone else's words (except for direct quotes), it won't resonate and your posts will fall flat. More importantly, Facebook has tweaked their algorithm in the last two years, so the system recognizes copied content and will limit its reach. Instead, use the content of others to spark ideas but make the words and sentiments your own.

Step 4: Share Yourself

People don't just buy products or services because they are out there for sale. They buy from people they know, like, and trust. Your network needs to connect with the *real* you and understand *why* you are in business. Your posts help people get to know you, understand you, and connect to you. To be really effective in the social media marketing space, you have to be willing to be authentic and vulnerable.

Have you heard of the Facebook Fallacy? It's the belief that other people have perfect lives because their social media feeds are perfectly curated and only show the very best of everything, avoiding all discussions of challenges or hardships. In this new "magnetic marketing" philosophy we can dispel this fallacy by showing up as our true and authentic selves.

Step 5: Create a Strategy

Think like a CEO, not a hobbyist, and get intentional about your business. Create a posting schedule and strategy using the content triangles discussed in Step 1. Each month, create posts that line up with that strategy. Post 2–3 times per day on each platform but don't post the same thing on every platform at the same time. Mix up your content so people have a reason to find you in other places. And remember: post no more than once a day about your business, products, or opportunity on any social media platform. When all your audience sees is "Buy This," they will learn to scroll past.

To make posting easier, you can use a scheduling program for Instagram, Twitter, LinkedIn, and Pinterest. Facebook posts, however, must be scheduled to your business page directly.

An easy way to mix up your content is to find 30 items you want to share over the next 10 days and list them 1–10. Post them in the scheduling program 1–10 on one platform and reverse the order on the second platform, going 10–1. If you use a third platform, start at content piece number 5 and go to 10, then do pieces 1–4. It may sound complicated but a scheduling program will make this fast and easy and you'll have engaging content on all your platforms. (P.S. Some scheduling programs let you schedule far into the future, so you can recycle your favorite posts once every 60 days or so to create less work for yourself long-term!)

Step 6: Increase Your Visibility

There are a few ways to increase visibility on each platform:

- Use emoji's in your posts. They increase engagement by up to 30%.

- Use branded hashtags to help people find you more easily. Create a few hashtags and research them by googling them or typing them into the Facebook search bar to ensure they aren't already being used, and that they line up with your branding. You might have to get creative but the upside is, they help people find you across platforms so the work is worth it.

- Go Live – Live video on Facebook is the best thing you can do to build your brand. FB Lives get ranked higher in the algorithm and they get announced to people in notifications, so leverage them often!

- Use Stories – Stories on Instagram and Facebook get a ton of engagement, so spend a few minutes each day loading up a story that creates interest and curiosity.

- Post links in comments – Facebook wants to keep you on Facebook as long as possible, so adding links in a post will get your posts "punished" and they will be pushed lower in the algorithm, meaning they will get shown to fewer people. To work around this issue, mention in your post that the link can be found in the comments section.

Step 7: Become a Subject-Matter Expert

Whatever field you're in, learn all you can to help educate others. Do your best to help someone else finds solutions to their problems in your field by making honest recommendations – and not necessarily for products or services that you sell. When people recognize that your number one goal is helping them, not merely making a sale, you'll raise your level of credibility. And that is solid gold in today's currency.

Step 8: Create Lifestyle Posts

There is so much more to being in direct sales or consultative sales than just the products or services you offer. These businesses are about helping people and building relationships, so incorporate your business into your life. Find new, creative ways to incorporate aspects of your journey in your social media posts. The key is to focus on the positives. No one wants to buy from a whiner, so stay upbeat and talk about the challenges you have overcome – the way your business feeds your spirit, increases your confidence and pushes you to grow into a new, better, more capable person. Share some of your favorite parts of your journey. Talk about the friendships you've made, fun travel adventures you've been on, the gifts you've received. Talk about your clients and how you've been able to help them; shout them out for being willing to try a new product, and celebrate their results and their successes. And lastly, celebrate your team. Build other people up by reinforcing their strengths, giving them confidence, and showering them with compliments and encouragement.

Step 9: Use Branded Graphics

Everyone loves a good quote or sassy text graphic. And we love to share them all over social media. Some have even gone viral. When you see something you like and it resonates with you and your topic triangles, you'll want to share it with your network. But before you do, think about this. When you share a graphic – especially a funny or motivational quote – it's typically branded for *someone else*. So you are leading people away from you and your content – and toward other people who offer great content.

Remember!

Because of copyright laws, it is illegal to add your logo and contact information onto other people's images. Instead, create your own text graphics and quotes... or buy them. Creating a number of graphics to share over the course of a month can be quite a daunting task. You'll need to research quotes on your chosen topic(s), find the right images, and build the graphics. It's not difficult but it can be time-consuming. Be sure to brand all images and text graphics with your logo so when you share them online, it leads people back to you!

The other alternative is to buy graphics that you can brand for yourself, saving you time and effort that can be used for other business-building tasks. And that's where my passion for quotes comes in...

I have created an online shop where you can quickly purchase bundles of graphics to meet your every need and topic. There are several sets of motivation and mindset quotes, bundled in different size packages. There are also quotes and text graphics for different industries including fitness, travel, beauty, and real estate. Lifestyle quotes showcase your personality and interests and the online shop includes quote images and text graphics on wide-ranging topics from coastal to fashion and glam, home, beauty, and girl power. And the Celebration and Shout-Out category of quotes includes text and image quotes you can use to celebrate the special people (and team members!), recognizing birthdays, special celebrations, and accomplishments.

The beauty of these graphics is that once you purchase them, you own them and you can quickly and easily brand them for yourself – or your team – and use them for years. Each package of graphics includes a branding tutorial video to easily walk you through the process of branding them with your logo, website and/or contact information. And since you purchased this book, you are eligible for a very special offer – 30 graphic quotes for just $7!

Get all the details right here at

ceotiptalks.lpages.co/book-offer-boss-brand-graphics-sales-page

Selling online through social media doesn't have to be complicated or hard. Using a bit of planning, you can create an effective social media marketing strategy to set you apart from the crowd and make you an all-star in your industry!

MIMI SHEFFER

"You can't fulfill your calling in your comfort zone."

MIMI SHEFFER is a wife, mother, community volunteer and branding expert.

Coffee Lover + Brand-Builder + Cheerleader for Women in Business

Well-versed in the art of juggling career, family, and purpose, Mimi understands how challenging it can be to rise above the busyness of life and create your own opportunities. She credits professional development for the ability to step out of her comfort zone and into a life of entrepreneurialism and options.

Now, fueled by passion and purpose, she is intent on empowering other women to start their own businesses by giving them the tools to effectively market, brand, and position their companies for success.

THREE HIDDEN STRESSORS
DESTROYING YOUR HEALTH...
THAT YOUR DOCTOR NEVER TOLD YOU ABOUT

RAY MILLER

I HAVE ALWAYS BEEN A HEALER. I am also a problem solver, but I never realized it until much later. From an early age, I had asthma that was so severe I was hospitalized several times during a five-year period. In eighth grade, I endured innumerable challenges in school and was depressed most of my teen years. Thus, at the age of 14 I started seeing a therapist who treated me without charge because he had never seen a 14-year-old wanting and needing answers as desperately as I did. I survived high school and beyond, and started addressing my physical health. I became a fitness trainer, changed my diet, and studied nutrition.

My acute interest in the body as a whole led me to pursue a career as a massage therapist, which naturally found me specializing in pain relief. After a brief period of time, I nurtured and built a successful practice. Although I was healing all of my clients with positive results, I knew there was more to pain than just the musculoskeletal system. I embarked on studying the nervous system and its role in all types of pain – emotional and physical. I studied various types of body work and movement therapies. My results with clients started to skyrocket, as I was addressing the root causes of their pain.

Yet, it wasn't enough. I was compelled to dig deeper, thus I trained to become a functional diagnostic nutrition (FDN) practitioner. My current work pushes me further and motivates me to learn everything about the body's internal health. As I continue my journey as a practitioner and a healer, I have become impassioned by results. When I work with a client, I understand the importance of not only treating the current source of pain, but also addressing the history that roots itself deep inside the nervous system.

I will never forget how I felt as that vulnerable 14-year-old seeking answers, learning about my own internal and external pain, and the relief I felt when I found a practitioner who knew how to help me – who cared to help me. And this is the type of practitioner I aspire to be for my clients.

Stress Kills, No Doubt About It

Plenty of research exists on stress and how it can negatively affect your health, happiness, and overall quality of life. An overwhelming amount of information is readily available. Managing external stress is critical for optimal health. Some approaches include massage, yoga, meditation, exercise, proper sleep, and nourishing relationships.

Types of stress discussed in this chapter are known as hidden or internal. These stressors occur internally and typically without our awareness. However, there is another equally destructive kind of stress: external stressors. We are all too familiar with this kind of stress – overworking, losing loved ones, and relationship difficulties.

The major problem with internal stressors is that they can cause myriad negative symptoms ranging from fatigue and headaches, to depression and anxiety. This can be perplexing to an individual who exercises, meditates, eats healthy, and gets sufficient sleep. These people are living well, but are not feeling well.

So the individual seeks a doctor for a checkup. Blood tests are returned. They are normal. This individual is treated for *relief* from symptoms. However, the root cause – or where the symptoms originate – is not addressed. And now the original health issue is worse. Providing pain relief for a broken bone and not setting it and placing it in a cast never cures the initial broken bone. And you're still in pain. You may feel temporary relief, but the problem will persist, the pain will worsen, and the broken bone will not properly heal until it is correctly treated.

Remember, not one system in the body works alone. To enjoy a healthy life, the goal is to achieve homeostasis, or a state of equilibrium in the entire body. Here are some of the most common internal stressors and how they could be affecting you.

Food Sensitivities

First, understand food sensitivities are not the same as food allergies. With allergies, there is usually a noticeable response – you often feel better. However, when you experience food sensitivity, you may notice immediate discomfort after ingesting a certain food; thus, it is not as overt as food allergies. Even if you do have symptoms, they may be delayed for many hours, but still create an inflammatory response over time. And this is what we seek to eliminate, as it is destructive to our system.

Even healthy foods such as broccoli, berries, and kale can be problematic if a person has food sensitivity to any or all of them. One person's health food is another person's poison. We are individuals and we require different health needs. Just because a friend or family member follows a certain guru or diet protocol and feels better, it doesn't mean you should follow their diet. Your system is unique and, therefore, your eating program must be tailored to your individual system.

Case Study

I had a client come in with chronic headaches that weren't getting better. When she came to see me, she had already tried dozens of medical and alternative therapies. Not only was she still in pain, but the pain was also worsening. She followed a regimen of a healthy diet, exercised five times a week, and managed her stress with yoga and meditation. Her diet was mostly plant-based, which included vegetables and healthy fats such as avocados. She tried to manage the pain with natural supplements such as Turmeric, a powerful natural anti-inflammatory. After a comprehensive assessment, I suggested she take a food sensitivity test. She didn't see why this would help, but was willing to try anything, so she signed on immediately. The results revealed she was highly sensitive to avocado and guess what else? Turmeric. So the exact food she was eating for optimal health, and the supplement she ingested to decrease inflammation, were essentially increasing inflammation, thus worsening her symptoms. Omitting the reactive food and supplements from her diet was a critical part of her healing.

This is just one small example. Other conditions that can be related to food-induced inflammation include:

- Depression
- Asthma
- ADD/ADHD
- Fibromyalgia
- Irritable bowel syndrome
- Ulcerative colitis
- Migraines

Feel free to contact me for guidance and a reliable test and interpretation. An effective way to begin is to eliminate these common inflammatory foods: dairy, gluten, corn, soy, eggs, yeast, and nightshades (tomatoes, potatoes, peppers, and eggplant). Be sure to monitor how you feel. If you still are experiencing symptoms, consider a food sensitivity test. This tests 150 common foods to which you may be reactive.

Pathogens in Your Gut

A deluge of information in the health community discusses how important our gut health is to our overall well-being. Digestion and absorption are critical to a balanced metabolism. If your gastrointestinal tract is disrupted, the symptoms include bloating, indigestion, and diarrhea.

Pathogens that can reside in the gut are bacteria, parasites, fungi, and yeast. If any of these pathogens are present in the body, they can go undetected for years. Parasites and bacteria – good and bad – are always entering our bodies at some point. However, the mucosal barrier – a strong protective wall – shields us.

The mucosal barrier is where most of our nutrients break down and where absorption happens.

It creates a physical barrier against internal pathogens anywhere between the mouth and the anus. It is also a chemical barrier, which is an additional defense to the physical barrier called Secretory IgA (SIgA). This kills pathogens that enter our digestive system. In a healthy person, chronic emotional stress, drugs, excessive alcohol consumption, antibiotics, and food sensitivities can break this vital barrier creating holes. This is called hyperpermeability or "leaky gut," allowing these organisms to reside.

When the body is in this weakened state, an ideal environment exists for bad bacteria and parasites to thrive. This further taxes the system, leaving it vulnerable for secondary infections such as fungi and yeast, which create more unwanted symptoms. And so it goes, until you receive the proper attention.

One of the major problems with pathogens is that they can cause symptoms that are far removed from intestinal issues like indigestion, gas, ulcers, and constipation. They can also cause symptoms including migraines, acne, insomnia, depression, and hormonal imbalances.

If you experience such symptoms, begin by managing your stress. We all know, when your system is already compromised, managing stress can be stress-inducing. Some helpful suggestions:

- Reducing excessive alcohol
- Decrease sugar intake
- Eat whole organic foods
- Get plenty of sleep

Trauma Being Held in the Body

Emotional trauma from childhood, car accidents, falls, assaults, and domestic violence may seem like external stressors. Initially, they are external. But under extreme stress, the brain's objective is not to process the memory, but to remove us from danger and into safety as quickly as possible.

A mom, who we'll call Mary, is driving with her small children.

She is late getting them to school, and she has a work project due in an hour and she's already running behind. From out of nowhere, a car plows through a stop sign and hits her car from the side. The driver was moving at 35 miles per hour, so it was quite a jolt and shock.

This is a traumatic event for Mary. She has been hit by a car and her brain's first reaction is, "Oh no, are my kids hurt?" After she knows they are okay, she checks herself and there are no major injuries. Then see assesses the car damage and immediately must fill out paperwork and a police report, and afterwards continue with her busy, stressful day.

Let's review. She was already in fight-or-flight mode rushing to drop off her kids and finish a work project. Thus, her body was tense. Her car was struck by a vehicle that weighs several thousand pounds, which is not a normal event for our bodies.

Question: When did our ancestors ever get hit by a vehicle weighing a couple of tons?

Answer: Never.

This is a traumatic physical event even without broken bones. And especially it's emotionally traumatic. In that split second, Mary's brain thought, "Oh no, danger. Are my kids hurt? Are they alive? Am I okay?" A few seconds later, she realized everything was okay and dealt with the technical part of the accident.

Her brain navigated from "Are we alive or badly hurt?" to "Let's fill out paperwork and move through our day." Mary's central nervous system did not properly or thoroughly process the severity of the accident. She did not have the luxury of time. The nervous systems *can* process this kind of trauma, but they needs sufficient time. In our 21st-century demanding and hectic society, time is never an option. Thus, our nervous systems take the hit time and again.

So what does this mean? Possible symptoms Mary may experience could include increased anxiety while driving, especially heightened when seeing cars at STOP signs. This stress places significant pressure on her body because stress hormones cascade each time Mary drives through an intersection. And now her cortisol (stress hormone) levels are elevated, which, in turn, creates myriad symptoms over time. Then, there is physical trauma. Mary's neck may not even hurt, but it is still a physically traumatic event, thus impacted by the hit. She may experience neck pain years later and not know where or how it originated.

The first question I ask clients when they come to my office in pain is: Did you ever have a motor vehicle accident? Most will say yes, but no one was hurt – meaning no broken bones. I can often be certain the pain they have today is related to the car accident they survived 30 years ago.

In my opinion, this is one of the most misunderstood areas of health, and a huge missing link to many health programs and regimens. One of the most important suggestions I may offer you is to educate yourself on this valuable topic. For more information on emotional trauma held in the body, read *Waking the Tiger: Healing Trauma* by Peter Levine, and *The Body Keeps the Score* by Bessel Van der Kolk.

When experiencing pain from a former physical trauma, and you need to release the discomfort, look for a *Primal Reflex Release Therapy (PRRT) practitioner* (http://theprrt.com).

I hope you find this information helpful and discover ways to enjoy a healthy, happy life.

RAY MILLER

RAY MILLER, FDN-P, PRRTP, LMT, is a functional health coach, Pain Relief Expert, and a Certified Functional Diagnostic Nutrition (FDN) Practitioner. He has helped thousands of clients relieve pain, and conditions such as digestive disorders, hormonal imbalances, and autoimmune issues.

His results: thousands of individuals have been helped to restore their optimal health.

He offers a free 30-minute initial discovery health consultation.

raymillerhealthcoaching.com

www.evolutionpxp.com

"CONGRATULATIONS, DOCTOR YOU!"

DR. RUSSELL STRICKLAND

THESE ARE THE WORDS MY CLIENTS LONG TO HEAR. They're the ceremonial close to the dissertation defense, and the culmination of months (sometimes years) of effort and a lifetime of dreams.

My name is Dr. Russell Strickland. I am the Founder and CEO of Dissertation Done, where we help working professionals achieve the lifelong dream of earning a doctoral degree by getting their dissertations done!

What is a dissertation? Well, doctoral students spend a few years completing classes and then another few (or several) years conducting research and writing it up in a book called a dissertation. When the student can convince a committee of 3–5 faculty members (called the student's dissertation committee) that their book is good enough, they get to hear those glorious words, "Congratulations, Dr. You," and they graduate!

But here's the thing: although the exact numbers vary from year to year and school to school, it's widely accepted in the academic community that only about 50% of doctoral students ever graduate. Only 50%! Of doctoral students! I mean, you've got to be a pretty good student to even think about enrolling in a doctoral degree program. Right? And then it's basically down to a coin flip whether or not you will graduate? So, what gives?

What if I told you the three things that stand in the way of most doctoral students finishing their dissertations are the *exact same three things* getting in your way whenever you try to attempt something new?

1. Not knowing what the hell you're doing

2. The self-doubt that comes with not knowing what the hell you're doing
3. Oddly, perfectionism

You see, very few doctoral students have ever completed a dissertation before. After all, for most people, earning zero doctoral degrees is just fine, so one is plenty for almost everyone else! It's important to understand that *not knowing what you're doing* is actually to be expected. And doubt often arises in these situations. But perfectionism?

We'll talk about those first two issues a little later, but for now, I'd like to talk with you about Dante's little-known Tenth Circle of Hell – perfectionism. Perfectionism tricks people who would otherwise achieve great things into tolerating lifetimes of mediocrity. It convinces some of the best among us to fritter away time and efforts on polishing surfaces few will ever see and fewer still would appreciate if they even noticed.

The French philosopher, Voltaire, observed that *perfect* is the enemy of *good*, although he said it in French, which, no doubt, made it sound even more pretentious. Fun fact: Voltaire was a significant voice in the Enlightenment movement of the 18th century, which was the impetus for the American and French Revolutions, later brought to the silver screen in *The Patriot* and *Les Misérables*. The three leads for these films all hailed from the former British penal colony of Australia. Collectively, they were best known for playing a Scottish revolutionary, a Roman gladiator, and a claw-fisted comic-book mutant who wouldn't die. I doubt Voltaire would have found this casting to be *perfect*, but 10 Academy Award nominations and three wins later, I bet he would have thought it was *good enough!*

I counsel all of my students to focus on their real goal, which is always graduation rather than the dissertation. The dissertation is simply a means to an end – a school project they must complete in order to earn the title, Doctor. That means that the real goal is to get the dissertation done as soon as possible, not to write the perfect dissertation!

You see, doing an exceedingly good job in school is exactly what gets most students into a doctoral program in the first place, but continuing that level of perfectionism is not the way out of a doctoral program – not a successful way out at any rate! So, I advise my students to remember that good enough is good enough.

One student, let's call her Gina, had a particularly hard time with this concept. She understood that the real goal was to simply get her dissertation approved so that she could graduate. She agreed that finishing sooner was better than finishing later... and certainly better than *never!* Her head was onboard, but her heart was a different matter. Her heart wanted kudos and praise for a job well done.

When I was in elementary school, the teacher would put a little foil star on your forehead if you'd had a good day. And if you had a really good day, you'd get a gold star! Getting a gold star was a great motivator for me in elementary school. Unfortunately, some of my doctoral students still crave that same validation. I tell them that the doctoral degree and title *is* their gold star. Although they tend to understand and agree, some of them never really accept that good enough really is good enough.

So, Gina had a particularly ornery dissertation committee member, as many students do, who we'll call Dr. Pain-in-the-Ass. Nothing was ever really good enough for Dr. PITA. Even when she approved a draft, her approval was always accompanied by some sort of dig or slight.

Gina struggled with Dr. PITA's demeanor. Whereas I wanted Gina to respond to the substance of her committee members' feedback and ignore any color commentary, Gina was upset by this particular committee member's constant derision. And, so it went throughout Gina's dissertation journey, until at last she was invited to defend her dissertation.

Now a dissertation defense sounds like a nasty battle, a knock-down, drag-out fight, but it's not. You see, your dissertation committee invites you to defend your dissertation only after your committee members have approved your work. They're simply not going to invite you to defend unless they fully expect you to pass your defense and graduate. Anything else would reflect badly on *them*. So, it's really more of a celebration than a tribulation. A coronation consummated with the ceremonial, "Congratulations, Dr. You."

That afternoon Gina called. I love getting calls from my students after their dissertation defense. I love celebrating with my newly minted Doctors, congratulating them on their accomplishments, and talking about next steps as they prepare to leverage their degrees to make our world a better place!

But when I answered Gina's call, I could immediately hear in her voice that something was wrong. How could she possibly have failed her defense? As I already explained, that just doesn't happen! Yet her voice trembled. "Dr. Strickland, I just didn't know what to say."

I asked what had happened. Now audibly sobbing, Gina continued, "Dr. Pain-in-the-Ass told me that mine was the least relevant, most marginal study she had ever approved. And I didn't know what to say!"

"You should have told her, 'Thank you'," I responded, relieved to learn that Gina had, in fact, passed her defense. You see, she had heard "least relevant" and "most marginal," whereas I heard "approved!"

Gina and I had agreed over and over again that her focus should be on getting her dissertation done... that getting the document approved was good enough, and that graduating was the reward – not compliments, pats on the back, or even gold stars! But even though we'd had that discussion time and again, even though Gina had agreed in principle, and even though she *knew* it was right, her heart still wanted that praise.

When she didn't get it, one of the best days of her life was dampened by a damaged person who took delight in belittling others. And, as much as I tried to cheer Gina up, to help her shake off the sting of Dr. PITA's parting shot, the day had already been diminished.

Dr. Gina did come around, though. I advised her to celebrate by calling all of her family and friends and saying, "Hi. This is Dr. Gina!" That certainly helped!

It's important that you give your clients (and yourself!) permission to not be perfect. Good is actually much better than perfect. Perfect separates the perfectionists from the rest of us; good helps the masses. Perfect takes forever; good can be delivered quickly. Perfect is very specific; good can be prolific.

So, we've covered why perfectionism gets in the way of achieving your goals, but what about the first two points I mentioned earlier? What do you do about not knowing what the hell you're doing and then doubting yourself because you don't know what you're doing?

Part of it does come down to mindset. It's perfectly fine – healthy, even – to recognize that you don't know what you're doing. But consider these two statements:

"I don't know what I'm doing."

"I don't know what I'm doing, yet."

The first statement reeks of resignation and despair. The second connotes commitment and resolve. What you say and how you say it (even to yourself) matters.

But ultimately, it doesn't matter how you say that you don't know what you're doing, if you don't find a way to remedy the situation. And that's why you need support.

One of my first students with Dissertation Done, Jamie, studied the types of support a student needs to complete a dissertation project. Specifically, Dr. Jamie focused on students completing their projects remotely, meaning away from the community one would find on a university campus. Most of her subjects were enrolled in online universities, just like her. However, some students had moved away from their universities' campuses after they began their dissertation research.

Dr. Jamie found that there were three types of support that were relevant to the success of remote doctoral students: operational, emotional, and practical. Operational support concerns what to do and how to do it. It's the answer to the "I don't know what I'm doing" concern. Emotional support involves empathy and motivation. It's how Dr. Jamie's subjects held feelings of self-doubt at bay. And practical support is all about creating more hours in the day or less noise and distractions.

Of these three types of support, operational and emotional support were found to be critical to dissertation students' success. Practical support was nice, but not necessary. But the really interesting thing was the interplay between emotional support and operational support, as some of my future clients would learn...

"Dr. Strickland, I need your help." The woman's voice was resolved, and I thought that this was a promising way to start a relationship with a new student.

But then she continued, "Last night I told my husband to shut up because he didn't know what he was talkin' about."

I furrowed my brows. *What was going on?* I wondered. I'd talked with thousands of doctoral students, and I couldn't remember a single conversation ever starting out quite like this. Must have been a wrong number, but she knew my name... My inner monologue was about to get into a heated argument with itself, but I had to say something. "I think you've got the wrong Dr. Strickland; I don't work with couples..."

"No, no. You're that dissertation doctor. It says so right here," she insisted.

"Yes. I am. But I really don't work with couples." I wasn't sure quite where this conversation was headed, but then I recovered somewhat and asked, "How can I help?"

"Do you want me to tell you what he said?"

I was still confused. "Sure, if you like..."

"Well, he told me that I was smart enough to do anything and that he was sure I could finish my dissertation. And that's when I told him 'Shut up! You don't know what the hell you're talkin' about'!"

"So, you see, Dr. Strickland, I need your help!"

At this point my confusion cleared, and I understood exactly what was going on. This student had wonderful emotional support from her husband, but she was right about the fact that he didn't know what he was talking about. He had never completed his doctoral degree. He'd never worked on his own dissertation. In fact, he'd never even considered enrolling in a doctoral program.

This man loved his wife. Cared for her. Respected her. He wanted to help in any way that he could. And when things are going well, sometimes wanting to help is good enough. During the good times, showing support and encouragement is helpful.

But when you're in trouble, when doubt creeps in, you don't want someone who's never dealt with what you're going through humming Bob Marley's "Everything's Gonna Be Alright" with a vacant, toothless grin. You want your confidence restored. You want to know what you can *change* to make things *better*.

You want someone who knows what you're going through… because they've gone through it, too. And come out the other side successfully! The funny thing is that *I* could tell this student the exact same thing her husband had, without any specific advice, and it would actually help. This is the power of being an expert! The mere fact that you have the experience of successfully dealing with whatever your client is currently facing gives that client hope.

Now, hope is not a plan; you also need to be able to tell your client what to do and how to do it. You need to provide a new way of thinking about the situation – a paradigm shift. No one gets excited at the prospect of working harder, working longer, working faster. If what they were doing was actually working at all, they probably wouldn't be reaching out for your help, would they? So, doing more of the same thing isn't the answer. But when you turn someone's problem on its head, that's exciting!

My doctoral students often come to me dejected because they've spent weeks, months, and sometimes years writing their dissertations without making any real progress. I tell them that the real problem is that they don't know what they're *doing*… literally! You see, schools tell students to start *writing* with the assumption that the writing will lead somewhere. That somewhere is supposed to be *doing* something to conduct new research, but students never actually think about what they're going to be *doing*.

Novelists don't write Page One without first creating their characters' backstories and motivations, understanding their locations, and developing their narrative arc. Yet, this is exactly what most doctoral programs encourage their students to do: "Pick a topic and start writing!" I call it the Bloodhound Approach to the Dissertation Process, because a student gets the scent when he picks a topic, then he follows his nose to see where it goes. Now, bloodhounds are amazing creatures, but they sometimes lose the scent. And you don't want to do that as a doctoral student!

So, I help my students flip the whole process around. Instead of being a bloodhound, forging ahead, hoping to find something before you lose the scent, wouldn't it be better to have a GPS? I help them choose their destinations, map out their paths, and stay on track and on time. It's a completely different approach that gets the student excited! I've shown them what's causing their trouble, demonstrated that how they're approaching their work is actually *creating* the problem, and given them a completely different *system* for reaching their goal.

Are you creating a new system for your clients or simply telling them to work harder, longer, or faster? Give them a new perspective, create a unique vision for their goals, help them see things differently, and they'll be excited to follow you!

Are you a working professional struggling through the dissertation process? Are you the proactive type who'd rather do things right the first time? Is there a doctoral student in your life who needs to get his dissertation done?

Visit http://GetYour.DissertationDone.com/BehindTheScenes to discover the best way for you to get your Dissertation Done.

DR. RUSSELL STRICKLAND

DR. RUSSELL STRICKLAND is Founder and CEO of Dissertation Done. His career included turns as a rocket scientist, investment banker, and management consultant before becoming America's #1 Authority on Dissertation Completion for Working Professionals. Dr. Strickland has taught, coached, and mentored thousands of students in the professional social sciences over the past 25 years, including service on dozens of doctoral committees.

Dr. Strickland's dissertation coaching follows a project-based model designed to keep students organized and efficient throughout the dissertation process. As a result, his clients earn their degrees in less time, saving tens of thousands of dollars in tuition and hundreds of hours in wasted effort.

Dr. Strickland is responsible for the inception of National Dissertation Day, an annual day of recognition of the hard work and accomplishments of our best and brightest. He is also the host of the Daily Dissertation Inspiration podcast and Dissertation Inspiration Radio on YouTube.

SuperBoomers are Back in Business!

Suzi Seddon

ONE DAY I WOKE UP AND SMELLED THE COFFEE. I realized life had changed almost overnight. Suddenly I was on my own again, like many, after a tortuous separation and divorce process lasting a ridiculous and expensive 13 years, coupled with a dreadful experience that gave me a serious dose of post-traumatic stress. I was utterly and totally, mentally exhausted and the biggest question swirling around in my mind was how on earth was I going to start over again and earn decent money at age 56? How was I going to restore my financial security and freedom for the future?

I knew I had lots of skills and experience but as I looked bleakly over my shoulder I wondered who would employ me in a serious capacity even though I'd had a big career behind me. It was a mixture of feeling over-qualified to be in someone's employ again and rusty on skills.

For a few years I had run a costume jewelry business but I couldn't get excited about it. Jewelry made in the Far East, in a factory by someone I didn't know, wasn't a great backstory for sales. I needed something much more rewarding.

So I took myself off to a careers consultant. That was my first big turning point. I wanted to know what type of job role I was really showing up to employers as today. I expressed my worries to the Consultant... "Who on earth is going to employ me? Should I re-skill? Should I go back to college?" After a long chat, he sat back in the chair and smiled. "Suzi, you've done so much... stop looking outside yourself for the answer. Everything you need, you already have." I was sent off to think!

I reflected long and hard on his words and realized he was absolutely right. This wasn't the time to study for a degree. I didn't have the 7+ years to invest and I certainly didn't have the money. I returned to see him a couple of weeks later with the outline plan for www.7secrets.co.uk

I wanted to pull together everything I'd learned in life (and how to survive it) and not least, how to live the best 100-year life. I have always had a curious mind, hungry for information. Friends said I should have been a doctor, and it's true I have always had a fascination for health and nutrition in all aspects. But I also wanted to do something meaningful not meaningless. Moreover I wanted to use the things I held passion and aptitude for to launch my 2nd Act – my SuperBoomer lifestyle. My Mum is 95 this month and is a real beacon for how to live the 100-year life. She was and is my inspiration as to how to do it. The more I contemplated my situation, the more I realized there were certain keys to getting things right. These I call the "7 Secrets."

Gone were the days I spent as a Yuppie in the 1980s, focusing my life totally on work and my career. Now I wanted balance, but underpinning *everything* I realized, is financial security and so I started to focus on creating courses to help others navigate the same path. If I could help just one person to avoid the pain I had been in, I would feel I had something really worthwhile to offer and I could also create passive income for myself.

My generation lives with a carefree attitude to life. If they have money, they are not afraid to spend it. "You can't take it with you!" is an oft-used phrase of the defiant Boomer who wants to live for today. However, it has also become screamingly obvious that we're all living a lot longer and that the money/savings will likely run out a lot faster. Add in the financial roller coaster we are riding wherever we live in the world, and that our children probably need our financial help, and that divorce rates amongst our generation are probably at the highest they have ever been, and it's no wonder that many need to re-ignite their ability to earn.

So what to do? Like others in my generation, I wanted to live life to the fullest while continuing to earn. What I needed to work out was how. I didn't want another office job 9am-5pm and I didn't see myself retiring early then living for potentially another 40 years with neither focus nor finance.

So my next breakthrough came when I realized I didn't have to re-invent myself. All I needed to do was create an audience to sell my media courses to. The problem was I didn't have any money for marketing. I had no budget. I couldn't afford to just buy "lists" like I heard others do. I was seeking a way to find an audience that was valuable but that I could create without any budget... and thankfully that's when I discovered Facebook Groups. I swiftly created and began to build my Group month on month. I learned how to write engaging posts, how to create Facebook ads, and I learned all I could about those who joined to see how I could help them and create a niche for myself. Now I had an audience I could monetize.

In tandem with my Facebook Group, I began to create online courses for people who wanted to repackage and repurpose their own skills and experience. One lady was an events organizer of some 30 years standing, another ran a Bed and Breakfast business, and there was a couple who wanted to coach business start-ups. Someone even wanted to teach people how to complete their tax return! The message came back to me loud and clear. Whatever skills and experience you possess, whatever walk of life you are from, there is somebody out there right now searching for you and you just need to find a way to re-package your skills to find each other. The beauty of selling your own course online is that it sells while you sleep, 24/7 x 365 days a year. That's what makes it so powerful.

We live in an extraordinary time. In the 1980s no one had the opportunities of selling across the world like we can today utilizing the internet and selling to our niche audience.

My next step was to do an Online Summit (also known as a live streaming event). I brought together seven business owners to discuss their success secrets on how to build and monetize wildly successful Facebook Groups – 604 people registered to attend online. Not only did I increase my email list of potential future customers, I also learned so much from running that event, both in the back office and the process of presenting live. I also learned a lot from the multitude of questions I had for all seven experts. Several have grown multimillion-dollar businesses, and Facebook Groups have played an important and on-going part in their strategies. Most use their Groups to invite people to get a "try before you buy" experience and get a taste of their presenting style, to get to know, like and trust them before introducing a well placed product, program, or service congruent to their audience's needs and wants.

I recorded my Online Summit and sold the recording (and still do). It is an amazing and on-going success.

Next I released my courses:

The FB Group Blueprint

This course outlines all the steps needed to create and build a Facebook Group of raving fans from scratch. It includes step-by-step instructions including plenty of "How to..." videos. I also cover ideas for creating engaging content and monetizing your Group. Remember the first thing you need is to create an audience, and this Blueprint tutors you how to build a *warm* audience that you can later sell your products, programs, and services to.

The Course Creator, Cash Maker

This course is all about taking your passions, knowledge, and skills and putting them into a course that can be sold and delivered online.

The fantastic thing about creating an online course is that it's a way to create value on scale. If you worked a traditional 1-to-1 model, you would earn much less money for doing much more work. Online courses allow you to reach students all across the globe and earn money (as the pitch goes) even while you sleep!

I particularly love online courses as they relate to "SuperBoomers." We've all gathered so much knowledge and (dare I say it) wisdom, during our "first acts," it seems almost wasteful not to share and profit from this knowledge in our "second acts."

The best thing is that it is relatively easy. Most of my students come to me not appreciating just how blessed we are with technology in our modern world. Just six years ago, you would have had to have a big expensive website, professional camera equipment, and a team of coders, video editors, and designers just to produce one simple online course. These days you can buy software packages that include video hosting, membership course creation software, marketing page creators, and even marketing email software, all for a low monthly cost. You can "hire" freelancers online to do design and tech jobs for one-off payments. It's a golden age for online course creators!

The Course Creator, Cash Maker course breaks everything down into 6 simple steps:

1. Finding your hero idea
2. Structuring your course
3. Creating your course
4. Marketing 1
5. Marketing 2
6. Delivering your course

The thing that most surprises people is how much they actually know! When we have a skill, we tend to forget what it's like to not have that skill. I believe the fancy term for this is *knowledge blindness*. This means that your head is a potential goldmine of information. You just need to recognize this and have a format for breaking everything down into easy-to-implement action steps.

I'd love to offer you a Free Gift to kick-start your course ambitions...

The Course Creator SuperBundle:

- 5 Steps To Create Your First Online Course Guide
- 5 Steps To Build A Thriving Facebook Group Guide
- Our Unique Content Marketing Planner
- Our Bonus Resources List

Just go to this link and enter your details:
SUZISEDDON.COM/SUPERBUNDLE

Today I work from wherever and I love it. I have the resources to travel and enjoy all sorts of experiences and live as a SuperBoomer who hasn't given up life for a pair of carpet slippers and the occasional break at the seaside. And I am here to tell you, if I can do it, so can you!

SUZI SEDDON

SUZI SEDDON, Digital Course Maven, started her entrepreneurial life with no special education or University degree and considers herself to be a student of life. She has worked across a number of industry sectors, predominantly in IT and computer video games, involved in taking products to market on mobile devices and digital TV platforms.

She is renowned for being a highly motivated, natural saleswoman, motivator, and creative thinker with an ability to distill complex information into simple-to-use roadmaps. Suzi thrives on understanding the dynamics of the communication of information in all its forms and has been instrumental in creating a number of online businesses and many courses over the years.

Today she has created her own branded system – The Time & Money Freedom Formula – which focuses on her own baby boomer generation mastering the essential elements required for launching their own digital course business.

www.suziseddon.com

Destined to Travel

Tami Santini

WHEN I FIRST OPENED MY TRAVEL AGENCY, I quickly learned that I was in over my head. The world of travel is just that – *the world*. Yikes! The only country other than the U.S. I'd been to at that point in my life was Canada.

Thankfully, my husband was wise enough to say, "We need a niche," and thus we focused on romance travel and honeymoons more specifically. Exciting, right? I loved working with these couples and quickly felt like a natural. While discovering my niche and finding my place in the travel industry got me off to a great start, it didn't take long for me to realize that I was clueless about being a business owner. I spent countless hours and thousands of dollars on the *wrong* stuff while I *thought* I was building my business.

I followed the so-called "experts" and found myself frustrated, exhausted, stressed, broke, and quite frankly ready to give up. Have you ever been there? I was working diligently and doing everything the experts said to do yet still felt like a failure. I had clients, but every dollar I made was going back into the business... so that I could stay in business.

After a few years of this, I was ready for a paycheck, you know what I mean?

Everything came to a head one Sunday evening. I just wanted to relax because I had been working a long stretch of seven days a week for several weeks in a row. But I couldn't take time off. My two daughters were on the gymnastics team and in order for us to be able to afford the team fees, we bartered our time and cleaned the gym every week. Demoralized, deflated, and defeated, I cried out to

God, "Why am I working this hard, investing so much time and money into my business and *still* have to barter my time? Is this even worth it? Should I even be a business owner? Should I get a regular job?"

I originally started my travel agency for financial freedom and flexibility. My husband and I were a newly married blended family of seven. We lived in a small three-bedroom one-bath home (yes, one bathroom for seven people), and he was a teacher plus deejayed weddings on weekends. Shortly after we were married, I lost my corporate America position that offered a great salary, bonuses, and company car. While cleaning the gym that Sunday evening, I couldn't help but think about the past and that job. I couldn't help but question my decision to work from home and build a business. I wanted financial freedom and flexibility, but I found myself overworked, underpaid, and not having any freedom or flexibility! Hello? Something was wrong with this picture, wouldn't you agree?

It was then that I felt prompted to look into the destination wedding niche. It was intimidating even though I was comfortable planning honeymoons. I knew what I was doing and how to talk the language. It was simple to work with a couple to plan a vacation, but I thought destination wedding planning would be so much more involved and would require more from me and would be harder and more time consuming... and, and, and.

Here's the truth... I was just afraid. I had the wrong mentality and I allowed the fear of the unknown to grip me and lead me down a path of struggle and resentment. I had heard about destination weddings and how group travel was profitable, but I didn't think I could do it. I didn't think I was capable. I didn't feel equipped. After my prayer/you-know-what-session, I decided to get over my fear and figure it out. Why? Because I was more fearful of staying where I was than trying something new and failing. I thought it was worth the risk.

Well, I'm happy to report that it *was* worth the risk. Not only was it a lot easier than I thought, but things finally started changing for me and my family. In a matter of a few short years, my life completely transformed. We went from barely getting by to paying cash for our vehicles, upgrading to a bigger home, paying cash for our daughters to go to college, going on bucket list vacations and being able to be generous on many occasions. Plus, I retired my husband from his teaching job, and he now works our business full time. God is good!

Why am I sharing all of this? Because I know there are a lot of business owners out there who are struggling... working around the clock, dealing with constant stress and responsibility overload, and that is no way to live! I want to encourage you to push past your fears and trust yourself. You will make some mistakes along the way and that is okay. It is how you respond to those mistakes and how you use them to keep pressing forward that matters.

This book is about secrets, tips, strategies and you're reading it so that you can learn from others. Well, let me go ahead and fess up to a very memorable *huge* failure and how it changed what I said "yes" to.

A few years back I was on a roll. I was at the top of my industry, known as the expert, getting found online with little advertising efforts and getting hired practically before people even consulted with me. "Wow, look at me! I'm so awesome! Man, I am absolutely amazing! I can do *anything!*" Then came the call from a potential new client who wanted to get legally married in Italy in less than three months. To be honest, I was hesitant, but she really wanted to work with me and really needed my help due to the time crunch, so I decided to send her a contract and invoice to hire me.

Before I go any further, at this point in my destination wedding business, I had sent people all over the Caribbean, Mexico, and Hawaii for their dream weddings and that was my wheelhouse. As a travel professional I had put together travel packages to Italy but never a wedding – especially not a legal wedding on such short notice.

Back to our story. A few weeks and *several* hours later, I hit a wall. I was going around and around with what the bride wanted. I was getting nowhere with finding availability and setting up the legal wedding, and I felt horrible. I was so upset because I really truly wanted to be an advocate for her and see this to fruition, but I was running myself into the ground trying to get this thing done while the rest of my clients were suffering as a result.

I had to make a decision.

So I decided to give her back the nonrefundable professional planning fee she paid me and call it a loss.

Not only was I beating myself up for failing my client, I was also beating myself up for taking the client in the first place, and then beating myself up some more for all the time lost with nothing to show for it! All that work and I gave her a refund from my "nonrefundable" professional planning fee! Oh gosh, this made me feel sick! I should have listened to my intuition when I was consulting with her. Why didn't I just say, "I would love to help you, but this isn't my area of expertise." Ugh!

Once I got over the self-pulverization of my ego, bandaged up my wounds, and put my big girl panties back on, I made a dedicated decision to start saying "no" to things outside my realm of knowledge. Hallelujah! What a newfound freedom I had discovered – the power of "no"!

Life is filled with lessons and sometimes we only learn them if we allow ourselves. To acknowledge failures and mistakes as an opportunity to create change is powerful. I had to look deep within myself and ask, "What were you thinking?" "Why did you do that?" "What could you have done differently?" Questions like these will move you in the right direction and get you back on track.

When I think back to the moment when I said "yes" to this nonideal client, I had to investigate what motivated me to answer that way. Was there a fear of lack? Was there a mindset of ego? Was there pressure to push myself to learn something new and become an expert at something else? I knew that unless I addressed these things, I might find myself in the same spot again in the future. Umm... no, thank you!

The truth is that in life we will face situations, we will encounter roadblocks, and we will come against adversity. The key is in how we respond. I'm a firm believer that what you put in will come out when you're under pressure. Because of this belief, I now have principles and disciplines that I live by so I can hopefully respond with grace next time and not react when the stress comes.

So, here are the secrets to my success, my nuggets of wisdom, universal truths that anyone can implement right away.

Dedication is Critical to Success

There are so many business owners out there wondering why they aren't making money on their side hustle. Until you make a decision that you want to be profitable and you will do whatever it takes – including staying up until 1:00 A.M. to finish a project even though you have a 5:00 A.M. wakeup call, spending your vacation time making videos, creating content and visiting other resorts so you can have more knowledge and better serve your clients, or returning a call to a client on a Saturday night – your business is a hobby. I'm not saying that this is your life all the time, but in the beginning, your business is your baby and you better give it all the attention and nurturing it needs until it can walk, talk, and brush its own teeth.

Discipline is a Good Word

Working from home has its challenges. For me, I've always had a consistent and disciplined routine and this is foundational because I'm not always motivated, you know what I mean? I've heard many struggle with working from home as they allow distractions like laundry and dishes interrupt work flow. This is not okay, in fact, this is a recipe for disaster. If you have a certain number of hours each day to get your work done, you have to pretend like you are in an office outside your home and you don't get to "go home" until you're done for the day.

You need to establish a consistent and realistic routine that will give you those office hours to churn out the work and will also give you time to be present with your family. If you have things hanging over your head because you got distracted for two hours in the afternoon, you won't be able to focus on your family when you need to. You might be there physically, but you won't be there mentally, and it will be obvious.

Set Your Hours

I will be honest with you. I'm not always the best at this. Depending on what is going on with my business (like when I have a lot of travelers or have emergency situations and my clients need my help), I can work late hours. This is going to happen, so don't beat yourself up about it. Owning a business isn't a 9–5 job. There is always something to do. As humans, we need to give ourselves boundaries so we can stay healthy, and we have to get our priorities in order. By the way, our priorities are always *people* and that starts with our *family*. Anyway, setting up regular hours allows your clients to know when you're available and lets your family know when they can expect you to be available for them.

Take Care of Yourself!

I cannot emphasize this enough! I exercise five days per week minimum. Do I want to take the time to do this? No, especially since I do some tough workouts. But what I found is that if I can push myself during a physically uncomfortable situation like a bunch of pushups, I can use that same grit to push myself past my comfort zone in my business goals.

Remember, if I don't take care of myself, how can I possibly take care of others and serve my purpose? Plus, there is no time to be sick as a business owner, so you have to be serious about your health. Eat a healthy balanced diet and if you're too busy to plan healthy meals, pay for one of those meal delivery services.

Drink a lot of water. Get a standup desk. I stand at least 50% of my day if not more. Take breaks. Go on vacations or mini getaways. Entrepreneurs tend to run themselves into the ground and the amount of stress involved in building a successful and thriving business requires some proactive habits to manage the stress and the responsibility, so take care of yourself!

Keep Learning

I have a daily habit of reading and spending time on personal development. Something is better than nothing, so don't get overwhelmed by this. Here's the scoop – challenges will come, and as you step out and build an empire, the challenges will increase, and so will the responsibility. Hooray! Thankfully, so does the paycheck – woo-hoo! It is imperative that you are consistently investing in yourself to continue to grow and develop new skills so you can handle what is required of you as a CEO. Go to a seminar or conference, get a coach or mentor, join a mastermind group, read daily.

Master Your Mindset

I could go on and on about this, but your mind will determine where you end up. If you are ever at a place in your life and business where you aren't happy, you have to address your mindset. It has its own GPS and is leading you to a destination whether you know it or not. Constantly check fear. Constantly check doubt. Start recognizing patterns of self-sabotage. Don't say, "I can't." Don't look back, always look forward. Believe in yourself. Get around people who inspire you, encourage you, and push you outside your comfort zone. Get comfortable being uncomfortable.

Begin with the End in Mind

Take time to dream big dreams and have big goals. Then start with that end goal in mind and work your way backwards to determine the steps you need to take to make it your reality. Consistently work on those steps and little by little you will overcome, you will conquer, you will grow, and before you know it, you'll reach your promised land!

I encourage you to celebrate yourself along your journey. This is a process. Anytime I needed to go to the next level in my business, I had to first go to the next level personally. I had to examine myself and my heart and be willing to change my habits or mindset first and then it all fell into place. If you want to go somewhere you've never been, you have to do something you've never done.

Do you love to travel? Do you love to make money? Why not do both and build your own successful and thriving destination event planning business? Register for my next livecast to learn more:

https://tami-santini.lpages.co/
how_to_build_a_thriving_destination_event_business/

Follow me on Instagram: @tamisantini

Follow me on Facebook: @destinationweddingcoach

TAMI SANTINI

Wife, Mom, Entrepreneur, Minister and award-winning Destination Wedding Planner, TAMI SANTINI is a coffee lover, Jesus lover and foodie who enjoys travel, reading, and long walks on or off the beach.

Her travel business has whisked her away to exotic locations where she's seen monkeys in the wild, soaked in native hot springs in the middle of a rainforest, jumped off a seaside cliff, explored underground caverns with bats, got kissed by a camel, fed grapes to iguanas, swam with the pigs and so much more!

Now she is sharing her success secrets with others so they too can stay in overwater villas in Bora Bora, swim with sharks and stingrays, or hum the *Jurassic Park* theme song aboard a helicopter while gazing upon the majestic waterfalls of Hawaii because... why not?

THE UNITED FAMILY SUCCESS FORMULA

DR. TERI ROUSE

"Promise me that you'll always remember:
You are braver than you believe, stronger than you
seem, and smarter than you think you are."

—Christopher Robin, Winnie the Pooh (by A.A. Milne)

YOU *ARE* STRONGER THAN YOU SEEM. I believe this quote embodies a powerful mindset that I encourage you and others to embrace in yourself and your family. My purpose is to help parents discover ways to create positive lasting change – emotionally, socially, and academically – for your children... and yourselves. Ultimately I help to build a *United Family*. I know how hard it can be, especially when you have a child with challenging behaviors. These behaviors impact many facets of your life, specifically socially, emotionally, and academically.

My story perhaps mirrors your own, or that of one of your friends. After a failed marriage, raising a daughter as a single parent, and struggling to make ends meet to cover basic needs while working at a minimum wage job, I finally felt like I was on the upswing. Fred and I were getting married. Kristen (my daughter) and Matthew (Fred's son) were going to live with us – a mini Brady Bunch. I was also starting a new job as a special education teacher.

The pieces had finally all fallen into place – new marriage to a man who believed in me, new home we could call our own, two kids, and a great new job in an emotional support special education class! New beginnings all around. A fresh start for everyone... or so I thought. My new family and new job came with new challenges... challenges that I never expected.

Unfortunately our new beginnings were not smooth for everyone. Matt's new beginning encompassed numerous detentions and several suspensions from school. His infractions included smoking on the bus, skipping class, and stealing a scale from the chemistry lab just to name a few. Arguments about homework and chores became a daily event.

Kristen would come home from school and hide in her bedroom. She wouldn't ask friends to come over because she anticipated the daily battles. Things finally came to a head with Matthew after a lengthy school suspension. We asked the district for a special placement so he could be more closely monitored. After numerous meetings, lots of arguments, and buckets of tears, our request was denied! How were we ever going to keep this up? How were we going to keep up with the detentions, suspensions, the arguments and paperwork?

Not only did we struggle with Matt's academics, we struggled socially because we were often not invited to places because of Matt's behavior. And we struggled emotionally because we were constantly fighting. We felt isolated and quite honestly we were exhausted. I am sure that Matt felt that way, too. He was angry and frustrated. We were at a crossroads and we felt like there was no place for us to turn.

The suspensions and detentions and other disciplinary actions continued until finally Matt had enough. He dropped out of school... three months before graduation. We were crushed. We felt that the system had failed him, but worse yet, we had failed in our newly formed family.

After Matt left school, I sought out other parents who had the same experiences that we did and I found there were no solutions – nor were there any supports. I'd like to tell you that there is a happy ending for Matt and for my family but there isn't. After Matt dropped out of school he moved away. We have little to no contact with him now, but I will tell you what I do know for a fact today: I know that he is not living up to his best self. He can't... he doesn't know how.

The only fortunate thing is that Fred, Kristen, and I have worked hard to become the best family we know how to be... together. This doesn't mean that things have been easy, because we are still a work in progress, but we are a family doing the best we know how. Of course we argue and disagree but we have learned how to communicate better with each other. We have a circle of friends and supportive family who have helped us get through all of the changes. But there is more to this story.

After Matthew left, I went back to school, worked my ass off, and earned a doctoral degree in Special Education and Positive Behavior Supports. With this education and the tools I acquired, I decided to make it my mission to help other families overcome the same struggles and heartache we had experienced. I didn't want another child or family to feel the frustration and anger and despair we felt. I didn't want any child or their family to experience the struggles, the arguments, or the school and financial stressors that go hand-in-hand with these behaviors. I wanted to give every child and their family the opportunity to be the best versions of themselves, individually and as a united family.

So... I started my company K I D S: Interventions & Direct Services where I initially concentrated on providing behavior and academic support, and strategies for very young children and their families – you know, catch them early. However, I quickly realized there was a huge gap in services for school-aged children and for young adults. This is what prompted me to expand my practice to include children of all ages. Unfortunately this revelation came too late to help Matt, but with all of my heart and soul I believed I could help other children and their families. I am glad that I have been persistent. And I'm very glad that I expanded my practice, because I have been able to make a difference for this expanded population.

So here are some important things for you to remember:

It is never too late to alter the course your child is currently traveling, so you can create social, emotional, and academic success for you and your entire family.

Although you are super busy and in spite of a lack of time, you don't need to spend months or years to accomplish success. There are things you can do quickly that will have incredible impact.

There is *hope!*

Am I going to say it is easy? No, it isn't easy! But it *is* so worth it.

With all of this being said, I want to share with you the 3 Pillars of Success that will help you to *visualize* what you want, *strategize* how to make that happen, and *harmonize* to take advantage of all the great things you can bring to life for your children and your family.

Pillar #1: Look into your crystal ball. Visualize what you *really* want for you and your family. You will begin to see where you are and where you want to get to be. You will discover how to face those challenges and go forward fearlessly. The greatest part is that you will choose when and where you are going to start. "Start what?" you ask. Start your transformation from *Fractured* to *United*!

Pillar #2: Next you will learn how to Trash the Tissues and strategize *how* you will move forward to create the long-lasting positive changes you desire emotionally, socially, and academically. You will discover ways to help your child and yourself change your mindsets, how to make and keep friends, *and* how to go from detention to Student of the Week! You will discover what you want to be able to do, where you want to go, and who you want to bring along on this journey.

Pillar #3: Finally with the transformation to a United Family in progress and harmony in your home, you will begin the process of living your best lives together and as individuals. You will gain insight into possible alternatives to expensive therapies and medications. You will find different ways to communicate at home, to schools, and in social settings, *and* you will discover how to celebrate everyone's successes and support each other when things are challenging.

Please let me share my experiences with Jamil as an example. Jamil was a sixth-grade student in a school where I was a positive behavior support coach. I saw him wandering the halls on a daily basis. He was totally avoiding the classroom. This meant he was not receiving the quality education to which he was entitled. He was acting out, and failing miserably.

His family could not afford expensive therapies. His grandmother was growing weary of the phone calls and reports coming from school. As time went on, Jamil's behavior escalated and he became physically violent toward his teachers and peers. Everyone was frustrated and felt that they had "tried everything." Long story short, I came to understand that Jamil was avoiding the classroom and acting out in frustration... because he couldn't read! Sixth grade and he couldn't read.

While it took some time, I gained his trust and found what motivated him. I showed him and his family *and* his teachers that I truly cared about all of them and that he was important and valued. I worked diligently with Jamil, his teachers, and his family. Together we began working on Pillar #1. We were able to help him visualize what he wanted to do and where he wanted to go. Jamil shared that he wanted to become a fire fighter. Wow! That is quite a dream. How was that ever going to happen? Well, if Jamil didn't have a goal – a vision for what he wanted to do – how was he ever going to get there?

Now that he had an idea of what he wanted to do, we were able to research how to make that happen. We also explained to Jamil that no matter what, he needed a high school education. He needed to get himself together and attend class if he really wanted to become a firefighter. The school and his family worked as hard as Jamil to help him be successful.

Next all of the stakeholders – Jamil, his family, his teachers, and school administrators – came together to implement Pillar #2 and come up with viable strategies. We created several plans that were put in place for home, school, and in the community. Then we tried different things. Some worked... some not so much, but in the long run we were successful.

Jamil started to attend classes more regularly and we helped him discover more appropriate ways to express his frustration and anger. Jamil began to experience small successes. When he was successful, we *all* were successful. Over time there was a huge change in his mindset. He actually changed his mind about himself, and now others are seeing the real Jamil – proud, productive, studious, valued.

Finally Jamil has put Pillar #3 in place. Today Jamil is doing very well in his high school classes. He has been volunteering at one of the local firehouses. He has been out on calls with other volunteer firefighters and loves what he is doing. Jamil is now an avid reader. He still struggles, but he now knows his own value. He knows his purpose and he is moving forward fearlessly, everyday living his best life and sharing his life with his family.

Let me tell you *why* I want so desperately to help you with this. I know that the educational system is taxed to the max and I *never* want parents to feel the soul crushing heartbreak and guilt of their child falling off the face of the Earth (been there... done that!). I want you and I want *your* child to want to go to school, feel confident, get good grades, go to parties, laugh joyfully... become the best version of themselves. But most importantly, I want you to *believe* that you and your children are worthy. You all deserve peace and happiness. You all should experience social and emotional wellness and academic success.

Listen, I know that you feel that you've tried everything! I get it. At this point, where are you going to turn? You and your child are struggling with poor academic performance, anxiety, frustration, anger, therapies, medications, yadda yadda yadda. Right?

So at this point you have two choices. You can do nothing. You can stay stuck in this cycle of isolation, poor academic performance, financial stress, and emotional distress... *or*... you can take steps to experience radical, positive, and powerful changes in your child's behavior so you can promote academic success, and social and emotional wellness not only for your child but for your entire family. And you'll be able to keep some cash in your pocket rather than paying for your therapist's beach house.

So let me give you an example of one of the steps to social, emotional wellness, and academic success!

Think about how you see your family now. Circle words in each row that describe your current state of affairs.

	Current State of Affairs
Socially	Isolated Targeted Lonely Ignored Left out Avoided Bullied Disliked Embarrassed Frustrated Stereotyped Confused Tantrum Hopeless Helpless
Emotionally	Tired Frustrated Depressed Tantrum Angry Hopeless Helpless Confused Lonely Ashamed Embarrassed
Academically	Dislike school Embarrassed Bullied Pressured Stupid Anxious Alone Isolated

	Targeted Lonely Ignored Left out Avoided Bullied Disliked Stereotyped Frustrated Tantrum Hopeless Helpless

Next circle words that describe how you would like it to be.

	Where we want to be
Socially	Included Organized Hopeful Helpful Energized Friends Sporting events and teams Community Strong Invitations Connections
Emotionally	Excited Supported Focused Calm Included Organized Hopeful Helpful Energized Friends Strong

Academically	Successful
	Included
	Hopeful
	Helpful
	Focused
	Calm
	Organized
	Supported
	Energized
	Friends
	Strong

Take a good look at the words you have identified. Hang that list somewhere you can see it as a reminder. This is the first step in visualizing what you want for you and your family! Now you know what you want! You have it in front of you!

Now you can begin the process of uniting your family by following the proven suggestion in the United Family Success Formula.

By the time you complete Pillar #1 you will:

- Know what you *really* want for you and your family
- Be able to face challenges... together
- Choose where to start your transformation from Fractured to United

When you complete Pillar #2, which shows you how to strategize, you will:

- Change your mindset about yourself and your family
- Learn how to make and keep friends
- Have your child go from detention to Student of the Week

And finally after you complete Pillar #3 which shows you how to harmonize, you will have the tools to:

- Find alternatives to expensive therapies and medications
- Experience better communication at home, with school, and in social settings

- Feel and be empowered as individuals and as a family

Remember! You and your family are worth it!

If you want to transform your fractured and struggling family to a *United Family* living the best life you can, please reach out to me at:

DrTeriRouse.com

There is a video for you to watch and an application for you to quickly complete. I would be honored to have the opportunity to get you started on the journey of transformation.

DR. TERI ROUSE

Through her own life experience, DR. TERI ROUSE noticed a need for families to come together. She has made it her mission to help parents take control of their child's behavior so that they can experience academic success and emotional and social wellness as a united family through the United Family Success Formula.

She developed Dr. Teri's Go Forward Fearlessly, Empowerment, Control & Success System, FECSS UP! Which is designed to help people break the shackles of fear, take more control of their lives, and move forward fearlessly for personal empowerment as well as achieving their ultimate destiny without guilt, fear, or confusion for their personal success in less than 20 minutes a day.

Dr. Teri is an international speaker and travels the globe every year giving presentations at various organizations including the American Horticultural Therapy Association, Division of International Special Education & Services and Educators Rising.

Dr. Teri works with various community groups and activities including The Council for Exceptional Children (CEC), "Light It Up Blue" for Autism, Walk Now for Autism Speaks: Philadelphia, and Lily's Loop of The Lily's Hope Foundation. She is an advocate for people with disabilities through her association with the American Association of People with Disabilities (AAPD).

EVERYTHING I EVER NEEDED TO KNOW ABOUT TALKING TO HUMANS I LEARNED FROM TALKING WITH ANIMALS

VAL HEART

WHEN PEOPLE ASK ME WHAT I DO, I tell them with a grin, "People come to me with their pet problems, and then I help the animals with their people problems."

I have the gift of gab... with animals. Called the real life Dr. Doolittle, I am the bestselling author and co-author of several books, including "Don't Screw Up Your Dog," and have been a featured expert on ABC, NBC, and Fox News, as well as in *People Magazine, My San Antonio, Great Day San Antonio* and many others. I've been solving problems with pets since 1993. Based on what I've learned from animals, I created the HEART System, a unique five-step program that works with every animal, every time, *including humans!*

Here's the thing most people don't know: learning how to talk with animals teaches you how to better communicate with people.

These communication skills work on all levels with both animals and people – physical, emotional, mental, and spiritual. One of my students said after attending a class that she'd learned more in that 90 minutes than she had in five years of therapy!

I didn't always know what I know now. I started out a lonely, only child growing up outside Austin, Texas. Highly sensitive and empathic, the animals were my best friends. I could trust them. They spoke to me, shared their hearts and minds, their insights and viewpoints about the world we lived in together. I felt at peace and happy with them, accepted and loved. I could be myself authentically, vulnerably, and know my Truth. They "got" me. And I "got" them.

It was humans who made me crazy. To my dismay, I discovered that humans *don't* always tell the truth. They have hidden agendas, unspoken requests and needs, and often lie outright not just to me but to themselves. People habitually manipulate, abuse, and bully other beings, people and animals. The confusing social experiences made me doubt my own knowing and distrust my intuition. Maybe I was wrong, and what I thought I knew was a lie.

As I imploded into a deep hole of hopelessness, fear, and despair, I became manically depressed by age 12, and suicidal by 15. On those dark nights of the soul, when I was in agony from the latest wounds of the day, I would sneak out to the stable after my parents went to bed. My mare, Maisie, would nicker softly in welcome. Throwing my arms around her neck, I would bury my face in her thick black mane, pouring out my heart to her as my tears fell.

She would patiently listen, then offer me the wisest of counsel. She would help me see the painful experiences from a different viewpoint, and from the new perspective things would make more sense. She would tell me her own stories; sometimes they made me cry in sorrow for her life as a horse. Other times she made me smile and even laugh through my tears with a joke.

Maisie saved my life, day after day after day until I got a job and left home. Many years and many animals and many many experiences with therapists, counselors, churches, healing, and spiritual explorations helped me become who I am today. I use everything I've learned along the way to help others as a way to pay it forward for humans and animals.

Animals are angels, teachers, guides, and healers. They are gifts on loan to us from God. Anyone can learn to communicate with animals because everyone has an innate intuitive sense that can be developed, deepened, expanded on, and improved.

How can animals teach you to better communicate with people?

Consider these first five Heart Wisdom Nuggets:

1. Learn How to Listen

Most humans can't hear what others are really saying because they are too busy reacting to what is being said. We are formulating our responses before the other person has even stopped talking. Lost in our own heads, we are trapped in the clutter of our thoughts, sidetracked by our overwhelm and emotions, full of our own inner chaos.

Animals hate it when people don't listen. They feel disrespected, overruled, and unimportant. They go away mad, suppressed and/or depressed. Have you ever felt that way? When you track what happened, often you'll find a deep level of disconnect that occurred when you weren't heard.

If you think that they can't tell when you stop listening, you're wrong. They feel it.

There are different layers of listening. Your goal is to become fluent in all aspects, for instance:

Physical listening is about body language. Face the speaker, maintain soft-focus eye contact, and match your breath with theirs. Open your arms with hands in a relaxed position instead of wrapping your torso or covering your chest in a defensive posture.

Subtle listening is about observing the energy, the flow (or lack thereof), and the underlying emotion beneath the words and body language. Research has shown that approximately 90% of all communication is non-verbal.

Notice the intention behind the communication – both yours as the receiver and theirs as the sender. Activate your intuition and your subconscious will alert you when the speaker is not to be trusted, isn't listening, or is not telling you the whole truth. Warning flags can also tell you when there is something wrong, you're in danger, or you are being manipulated.

2. Be Fully Present

Animals are always in the present moment. They don't understand a human being stuck in the past, or projecting into the future. Humans can get so busy in their heads that they forget to breathe. People who are not present cannot be trusted.

Animals know that if they are not fully present then they are in danger of being eaten by the lion. When you are not fully grounded and focused in the present, then you are not paying attention. You are disconnected, with yourself and others, missing very important things that you would have caught if you'd been present.

We cannot communicate at the heart and mind level when we are not present. When we can't connect, we can't understand each other, and miscommunications and misunderstandings will happen on many levels. We are out of alignment.

When someone is talking, do them and yourself a favor by stopping your mental chatter and give them your total focus. Carefully consider what they are saying. Observe and lovingly witness them from a neutral, observer mode. No judgment. No criticism. Simply be present and listen.

Does something they say spark a thought or idea? Notice it but don't hook onto it. Thoughts can be like runaway trains. If you jump on the track you can get run over. If you grab on, it will drag you away. And if the bridge is out ahead? Then that's a problem.

Remember that you are a spiritual being having a human experience, and stay in a quiet, mental, emotional space. You'll be more present and a better listener for true understanding and aligned self-expression.

3. Ask the Right Questions

Asking the wrong question at the wrong time or in the wrong way won't get you very far. It can stop you in your tracks or take you in the wrong direction entirely. And as they say, when you're going in the wrong direction, more speed doesn't help.

Forgetting to ask the right questions in the right way and with proper timing is one of the most common mistakes my coaching students make. They wind up feeling blocked, limited, or stuck in their communication exercises with animals. It happens all the time with people conversations, too.

Consider the seemingly simple question, "why." Some coaches recommend asking "why" a minimum of five times before you can even begin to get to the heart of the matter. After you've connected and greeted each other, ask them to tell you their story.

When they are speaking – and you are practicing listening with your whole heart and mind, with focused attention – try asking "why is that important," or why they would say whatever they said. From a space of curiosity, wonder, acceptance, and open engagement without judgment or criticism, ask "Why do you think that?" or "Why does that matter?"

The first answers you'll likely get to the question "why" may be superficial or politically correct. The next answer could elicit evasiveness, or trigger a stronger emotional response... along with more interesting revelations.

Finally, if they trust you enough – if you've listened well enough, which fosters trust – they will tell you their immutable truth and you will know what weighs most heavily on their heart and mind. When you reach this point the energy changes. They may take a deep, courageous breath, and they may have tears in their eyes or their voice will change.

Ask and as always, *listen* from your heart space more than your head. Be compassionate, connected, kind, curious, and truly interested in them. If you feel triggered in any way be honest and tell them, explain *why* you feel the way you do.

Animals don't care what you're feeling as long as you're honest and clear about it and don't try to hide your feelings which makes no sense from their viewpoint. Honestly, it's impossible to hide anything from an animal. They feel and see it all, and they understand anger, stress, grief, sadness, fear, anxiety, and depression.

They don't understand suppressing feelings or pretending to be okay if you're not.

When you do that with humans, they will register consciously or subconsciously that you're being dishonest, you're withholding, or that something is wrong.

Part of our lessons on this earth are about healing fractured splits in our psyche. To become *whole*, aligned in harmony and congruent within. Some of us are more fragmented than others, but we all have our wounds.

Let the emotions roll up and flow over you like water over a rock in the stream. Be gentle with yourself and them.

With animals, if you demand answers to the questions you consider important without listening and understanding what's important to them, they won't talk to you. If you push them too fast to engage with you in the direction you want to go, before developing a proper trusting relationship with them so they feel good with you and are willing to give you a chance, they will simply block you out or ignore you. They may resort to a physical attack or run away. People do the same thing.

Do this right and you'll find others eager to talk to you. They will feel heard, respected, and safe. They will open their hearts to you, as well as their minds.

4. Set Your Intention and Detach from the Outcome

What do you hope to get out of the conversation? What would be the best possible outcome? Consider carefully before you engage in the conversation. Sometimes the most important part of a conversation is discussing what you both want to get out of your time together.

A magical thing happens when you get crystal clear on what you want. When you ask for it in your heart and mind, your request(s) guides the Universe, God, Angels, guides, and the animals so that what you need and are asking for help with can be revealed. Then all you have to do is show up, pay attention, and participate. Engage!

Equally important after you've set your intention is to detach from the outcome. Set your goals, wishes, and needs aside so you can observe and witness from a proper space of being unattached to the outcome. The answers you seek may not come in this conversation, but they may come later or from a different direction or source. Be open.

You may see the answers later on a billboard, on social media, in a book or a show. A chance encounter with a friend or an overheard conversation could show you the way.

Before you go to bed at night, task yourself by asking for what you want or need. Then let it go and leave it with your subconscious mind, God, and/or the Universe, while you drift off to sleep. When you wake up, reflect on the question you asked and see if your dreams or out-of-body night travels brought you back the answers you seek. Go on about your day with your eyes wide open, paying attention until you discover the answers you were looking for. Be open to receiving it from anywhere, expected or unexpected sources.

5. The Role of the Human/Animal BodyMind Connection

Animals mirror their caretaker's wounds, stress, illnesses, and imbalances. This is the hidden secret about animals that less than 2% of all animal lovers know anything about. It is the deeper truth to building a new level of communication and understanding between you and others, animals and humans, too.

Your animals know you better than almost any other being on the planet. They see what's in your mind's eye, they feel what you're feeling, and they can get closer to your heart than anyone else because they get under your defense mechanisms. After all, where else do we get unconditional love?

When we are in denial, or our emotional wounds are deep beneath the surface of our subconscious mind, the world around us will mirror these issues back to us. When we are emotionally disturbed, our animals and our children will often act out or react to our distress in different ways.

More than 90% our problems, both animals and humans, are based in emotional, spiritual, psychological, or psychosomatic issues.

It doesn't mean that all the problems are your fault, or that you're responsible. Other beings in our lives mirror us – people too! We travel in soul groups, and often come back together lifetime after lifetime to work on evolution as a "team" sport. Sometimes we choose animal bodies, sometimes we are humans.

The point of this concept is to consider an alternate way of looking at things. Because when you nail the underlying issues and *get* the lessons, then everything can change. Others help us in this journey to awakening consciousness.

Today many animal healthcare providers have seen a correlation between stressed, imbalanced, sick human caretakers and their sick, stressed out, imbalanced animals.

Often others reflect back to you your own imbalances and dysfunctions which, of course, drives you crazy. Then you think it's about them when all they are doing is mirroring a problem for you, acting as a teacher and guide for your soul and life lessons.

In Conclusion...

Animals are spiritual teachers, and at times, take on the role as the barometer for your soul. So anytime you have a problem with someone, and throughout all aspects of your relationships with others (human or animal), know that they are communicating with you on all levels.

Bottomline, the questions are: Are you paying attention? Are you asking the right questions? Are you fully present? Listening with your heart, not just your mind? Get this right and everything changes for the better.

Discover more principles of heart communication in my free ebook, *Hidden Secrets to Communicating with Pets* and improve your communication skills with people too! Visit:

www.LearnHowToTalkToAnimals.com

VAL HEART

VAL HEART is called the Real Life Dr. Doolittle™ and Animal Communicator to the Stars. She is the bestselling author of "Don't Screw Up Your Dog," which was #1 in its category, and has been a featured expert on ABC, NBC and Fox News, *People Magazine, My San Antonio*, and *Great Day San Antonio*. Featured on the cover of the *Spirited Women's Magazine*, she also won the Million Dollar Pet Pix award. She has been a regular columnist for the *Enjoy Whole Health Magazine*, and a contributing writer to *Natural Awakenings, Species Link Journal* and *Austin Pets Directory*.

She is the founder of the HEART System, a five-step program for solving problems with pets at www.ValHeart.com and www.ShowHorseExpert.com. She also founded The Heart School of Animal Communication and hosts the best online Animal Talk Coaching & Mastery Club at:

www.LearnHowToTalkToAnimals.com

If you've ever wished you could just put a microphone into your pet's head so you could know what they're thinking, then get ready to transform your relationship with your pets – and yourself – forever.

The Five Celebrity Steps to Building Authority in Your Niche

Brad Ross

BEING VIEWED AS A CELEBRITY or an authority in your field is important because it immediately sets you apart from your competitors. When you think of Internet search engines, Google is the first word that pops into your mind. Facebook immediately comes to mind when you think of online social networks, and Apple is top of the list when smart phones and tablets are mentioned. They all have what I call the *It Factor*. They are known, liked, and trusted.

All of those companies have been around for some time. They have worked very hard to develop customer loyalty. Longevity is often important in helping a company build a reputation as the leader in a particular marketplace. However, this is not always the case. Thanks to global Internet access and the World Wide Web, even a small, brand-new company can quickly develop an authoritative presence in just about any field ...

... if they follow a proven path to success.

How can you or your company benefit from the respect and admiration that comes with being an influential leader in your market, even if you are just starting out? Stick with me, I can help you.

Well, since 2004 I have helped entrepreneurs to establish themselves as the celebrity in their market, to close more sales and make the kind of money they deserve. I have grown my own influence and authority in multiple niches both inside and outside of the entertainment business as a professional entertainer and illusionist. And I was able to skyrocket my career from an unknown kid-magician, fresh out of college to making an executive level income touring the world and headlining in my own multimillion-dollar production, produced by Disney called Disney LIVE presents Mickey's Magic Show. I was cast out of thousands of hopeful magicians to star on this world tour alongside the world famous Disney Characters. It was Mickey, Minnie, Goofy, and Brad! Yeah, *Brad!* No, I wasn't wearing a furry costume... the producers booked me because I had the "It Factor" that they were looking for. I manufactured and created celebrity, authority, and expertise in my small niches that made me a proven entity that Disney could trust. How cool is that?

So, if I could go from making rabbits appear and twisting balloons into dogs at local birthday parties to performing at Madison Square Garden in NYC and the Dolby Theater in Hollywood... you can learn to stand out and become seen as the celebrity in your niche, too!

Over the years I have developed several proven strategies to shorten your path to becoming a celebrity and authority in your niche. I've assembled five actionable steps to help you start building your reputation as a leading influencer in your marketplace.

1. "Niche Down" and Focus

No matter what business you're in, you can learn a lot about becoming an authority figure in your field from someone like NFL Draft Expert Mel Kiper, Jr. Even if you don't care for football or sports in general (and I really don't, LOL), the following story illustrates how anyone can go from a "nobody" to the global leader in a targeted market in a very short period of time.

In the late 1970s in Baltimore, Maryland, Mel Kiper, Jr. was a teen-ager who loved the National Football League (NFL). The NFL is the largest professional football organization in the world. Kiper wrote player evaluation charts, showing what college football players he thought would be a good fit for the NFL.

The problem was, he was a total unknown, and no one took him seriously.

While attending school at Essex Community College in Baltimore in 1981, the young entrepreneur nevertheless started Kiper

Enterprises, calling it an "NFL Talent Evaluation Business." When anyone asked him his name, he would say, "Mel Kiper, NFL draft expert." The NFL draft is the process by which teams select college football athletes to play for their franchises.

At that time, there was no such thing as an NFL draft expert. Very few people paid attention to the draft, except if you were personally associated with college football or NFL teams. Not to be swayed, Kiper continued releasing a yearly draft report, and talking up the importance of his evaluations for the annual draft to anyone and everyone who would listen.

A young and emerging ESPN television network hired the self-professed draft expert in 1984. He tirelessly suggested to the growing 24-hour sports network that they needed to start covering the NFL draft before anyone else did. You can see where this is going. Today, thanks to Kiper's efforts in establishing himself as the preeminent authority in his field, the NFL draft is a multimillion-dollar franchise, which draws year-round attention from football fans and media channels.

And guess who is viewed as the top global expert?

That's right: Mel Kiper, Jr.

Kiper could have called himself a college football expert. However, that was a huge field, with thousands of individuals who were extremely knowledgeable about college football, maybe even more so than Kipper. His knowledge of the NFL meant he could have sold himself as a National Football League expert. The same situation existed there, with too much intelligent competition.

So *he* did what *you* should do.

He dug down deeper than anyone else, and found a niche which no one else was serving. He also ensured that he focused on an evergreen business.

Evergreen markets are viable year after year, providing a lifetime of revenue and profits to the authority figures in those marketplaces. While you can't foresee huge changes in technology, at least try to focus on markets that don't change from year to year. As an extreme example, centering your business around this year's iPhone model will limit your authority to the period of about a year. However, becoming an expert on all things related to iPhones and iPads would at least keep you evergreen while iPhones/iPads are still being sold, which will be a long time coming. You just have to stay on top of all the changes.

Fans of both college and pro football, NCAA and NFL executives, coaches, managers, and owners, as well as prominent college and even high school athletes were Kiper's target market. However, by placing a laser focus on a small niche market (the NFL draft), rather than a large market (the NFL or college football), Kiper became the #1 NFL draft expert "overnight."

Your lesson?

Don't sell yourself as just another dog trainer. Begin calling yourself the world's greatest trainer of Bichon Frises. Don't open a hot dog stand. Sell vegan hot dogs, served on almond flour buns, with a wide variety of natural, organic condiments and toppings.

Niche down far enough in your market or area of expertise and you will find a group of rabidly enthusiastic prospects who are being under-served. This is possible in any and every market, and can dramatically shorten your path to being viewed as an authoritative influence in your field.

2. Communicate with Stories

You just saw me demonstrate this. The above example about Mel Kiper, Jr. and niche marketing was relayed through a story. Storytelling has been used to record human history long before writing was even developed. Stories are still very powerful today, and I'd argue they're even more important. You can connect with people on an emotional, mental, and even spiritual level if you learn the art of storytelling.

You may be thinking your products and services don't have any heart-pounding, eyebrow-raising, dramatic stories surrounding them. In most cases, you would be wrong. Consider the case of the advertisement which has made more than $2 billion dollars for the *Wall Street Journal*. (Yes, that is billion, with a "B.")

It begins like this...

> "On a beautiful late spring afternoon, 25 years ago, two young men graduated from the same college...
>
> They were very much alike, these two young men. Both had been better than average students, both were personable and both – as young college graduates are – were filled with ambitious dreams for the future.
>
> Recently, these men returned to their college for their 25th reunion.
>
> They were very much alike. Both were happily married. Both had three children. And both, it turned out, had gone to work for the same Midwestern manufacturing company, and were still there.
>
> But there was a difference. One of the men was manager of a small department of that company. The other was its president."

The ad goes on to show that the only difference between these two young men was that the company president read the *Wall Street Journal*, and the other man did not. (Search for "Martin Conroy Wall Street Journal ad" online and you can read it in its entirety.) It's a great example of how storytelling can be used effectively for any product or service. I mean, *what on earth* can be more boring, less sexy, and further down your list of priorities than a newspaper subscription? However, because a compelling story was used to connect with its target audience, this short two-page advertisement was used for decades because it was so effective in showing the *Wall Street Journal* as the leading market influence for business and financial news.

In short, start using stories to communicate your personal or business message whenever possible.

3. Be Helpful

"Helpful? That's Brad's # 3? How will that make me into a celebrity in my niche?!?"

Have you ever sought help from someone who was really knowledgeable in a particular area? Of course you have. We do it all the time. When someone answers a question, or solves a problem that has been bothering you, you instantly look at that person as an influential figure. After all, they provided you with a solution you could *not* obtain on your own.

So yes, *helpful* is a huge part of being seen as an authority and celebrity. When you help someone with something they have been struggling with, you are now viewed by that person with a sense of respect and admiration.

Think of it like this – have you ever been sick with a stubborn bug for days or weeks not knowing "what you have." You finally decide to go to the doctor after everything you have tried over the counter hasn't worked. The doc performs his examination and does some tests. He determines you have "XYZ" and all you need to do is take this antibiotic for five days and you'll be fine. You *instantly feel better*. You haven't even left the office but in an instant his expertise has helped you and you see him as a hero. A hero who *helped you.*

Your goal should be to do just that – and be the hero helping people within your niche. In fact, that should be your job if you want to build your range of influence. Join forums relative to your market. Join, or start your own, groups on Facebook, LinkedIn, and other social networks where you can share your knowledge and expertise with others in your field.

Put your mind in a place of selflessness and deliver value *first* without wanting anything in return.

Don't worry about sales and profits for a little while, and try not to have a sales-only-oriented mindset. Just offer advice and valuable content that does one of these two things for your prospects:

1. Relieves a pain
2. Delivers a pleasure

Every important decision a human being makes is hinged upon either relieving a pain or delivering a pleasure.

So focus on developing, creating, and publishing helpful content online and offline that solves a big problem, or creates a pleasurable experience for your market. Your niche influence will grow, as will your reputation as someone who truly cares about others. That is certain to set you apart from others within your industry.

4. Build Strong Relationships

Who are the most important people in your life? Are they strangers, people you know nothing about? No, of course not. The people that matter the most to you are those that you have developed strong relationships with.

Because of the way you feel for them, these people have a very strong influence over your actions.

Becoming an important industry influencer requires building quality relationships, just like you do in your personal life. This can mean hard work in some cases. Think about your most important and valuable relationships with family members and significant others. They probably require a little work from time to time. They are not effortlessly maintained.

Take the necessary time to build deeper relationships with other industry influencers in your market or niche. If you connect on a very real level with someone who is seen as a market leader, by proxy you are also viewed as an important force in that marketplace. Other influencers are not the only people you should be developing rich relationships with, however.

Your customers, prospects, and anyone else in your field should be the source of your relationship-making efforts. Get out there, making yourself visible to anyone and everyone in your niche. Once you make an initial connection, do more listening than talking, and make sure you provide more "give" than "take."

Just a handful of important relationships can help you weather any storm that comes along in your industry. Your colleagues and clients will go to bat for you, want to see you succeed, and become your raving fans. These relationships are often a great source of business partnerships as well, which can further the influence of both parties in your market.

5. Grow Your Knowledge and Expertise

Finally, *keep learning and growing.* Take a minute and think about the people you consider authorities and leaders. You undoubtedly think of those people as knowledgeable experts, no matter what field they're in. This is how you must strive to be viewed in order to effectively paint a picture of yourself as a market influencer.

True leaders never stop learning. They thirst for knowledge and information concerning their field of endeavor. They want to be on the cutting-edge of innovation, technology, marketing, sales, and every other aspect of their business. Accordingly, they spend a great deal of their time talking to other leaders in their field, attending seminars and conferences, reading trade journals, taking new courses, and devouring any and all industry information they can get their hands on.

If you are in an especially competitive field, the right knowledge can revive and save your business. If you get hold of a piece of information before any other industry influencers or competitors, you have your hands on a potential golden goose.

Procurement of knowledge also means improving your skills.

You know what business areas you need to improve upon. Don't spend time working on what you are already proficient at doing. Brush up on those skills and market areas where you aren't so strong. Combined with industry knowledge and a constant effort at working to become better in your market, a well-rounded skill set can ensure you are viewed as an important influence in your field. Tony Robbins says it best...

"If you are not growing you are dying."

Conclusion

My Five Celebrity Action Steps will go a long way toward building your authority status. Smart business owners and entrepreneurs target a smaller, well-defined market rather than a broad one, using stories whenever you can to deliver content, information, and sales messages that connect with your audience on a very emotional level.

You should always be asking, "How can I help my market?" When you solve problems and help individuals with problems in your niche, without initially thinking about sales and profits, you develop strong relationships. Those relationships build your influence as your prospects, clients, and customers share your message *for* you.

Finally, continually learning and staying ahead of the curve in your market or niche is extremely important. People respect knowledge and expertise. You should always strive to be the go-to expert with the most relevant and actionable knowledge in your field.

These are just a few important pieces of the market influence puzzle. Consider them valuable tools in a large, well-equipped market toolbox.

If you'd like to learn more about becoming *the* celebrity in your niche, the authoritative market influence, and be recognized as the ultimate leader in your field, be sure to check out my complete course on How to Become an Industry Influencer & Celebrity and our 4-day live celebrity marketing Boot Camp – It Factor LIVE – which you can learn about at ItFactorLive.com

BONUS GIFT! I have The Most Epic, Valuable & Totally Free Gift Ever waiting for you right now. This FREE toolkit contains over $547 worth of powerful marketing tools and resources to help you easily stand out with your marketing, get noticed even if you exist in an overcrowded space, and get recognized as *the* celebrity in your market. To claim The Most Epic, Valuable & Totally Free Gift Ever TOOLKIT – head over to my website at:

BradRossMarketing.com

BRAD ROSS

BRAD ROSS is an internationally renowned speaker, illusionist/magician, author, marketer, and business success coach. He has been featured on over 500 national and international TV programs, trusted by major corporations like Disney, Six Flags, Universal, Aflac, General Electric, and Marriott. He has spoken on stages around the world in more than 36 countries, on five continents and has impacted millions of lives with his unique brand of magical marketing. On a personal level Brad is a competitive natural bodybuilder who enjoys fitness, cooking, and live theater. He's a Seinfeld Mega-Fan and a devoted doggy daddy to Merlin, an adorable Bichon Frise ball of fluff!

To get to know Brad better and connect, find him on social media @BradRossMagic.

Conclusion

Kim Walsh Phillips

I COULDN'T BELIEVE WHAT I HAD HEARD as we went around the room of attendees at our last Inner Circle Mastermind Meeting, getting updates from members on their biggest win since their last meeting, I held back tears.

You see, they had nothing a year ago.

This group hadn't even been formed yet. Nothing had been taught. No action had been taken.

And now, as the ocean waves crashed and the sailboats passed outside of our meeting room window...

- Lou and Tami Santini kicked fear in the patootie and launched their dream signature course, Your 20k Wedding Day. They teach wedding planners how to become destination wedding planners to multiply their income and reduce the hours worked. And their market said, "Amen." They've sold their course 63 times in less than four months. And they launched their first membership site with their founding members.

- Not allowing the desire for perfection to keep him procrastinating, Dr. Russell Strickland has brought in over six figures from his digital course funnel since January and just had a 75% close rate this week on his webinar. 75%! He helps doctoral students get their dissertation done faster.

- Mike Ski, a private investigator who went out on his own, went from a salary that kept him broke, to a multimillion-dollar firm, sold out his first boutique event, and got message after message from his attendees on how it impacted their lives.

- Magda Casteñeda launched her digital course, a healthcare certification, in the last 30 days and sold 34 at $2,500 to $3,000 each. Not only has she multiplied her income but she's able to serve so many more than she ever thought possible.

None of this existed a year ago.

None of it.

Yet, they all took action not knowing exactly what would happen next.

Tony Robbins says often that people overestimate what they can do in a year and underestimate what they can do in a lifetime. From this event, I am certain people underestimate what they can do in a year as well.

None of them knew what was in store, but they moved forward anyway. And now, a year later, they are changing not only their lives but the lives of those they serve.

God's plan + your purpose + a blueprint to follow... this changes everything.

If you have ever been asked if someone can "pick your brain." If you've ever been taken out for coffee to give someone else advice. If you have ever consulted on a project, program, service, or problem of someone else...

You are an expert. And there are people waiting to hear from you right now about your expertise.

This can be leveraged in multiple ways, such as:

- One-on-one coaching
- Group coaching
- Mastermind
- Digital course
- Online workshop

- In-person workshop
- Seminar
- Ebook
- Podcast
- Facebook Live Series
- Blog

And so much more.

You've just read about the experts in this book. You've taken strategies you can use over and over again to launch your message, grow your sales, and scale your business.

The way to take this from dream to success is to take action right now. After all, the only things made to blend in are baking powder and lizards, not you.

For you, my friend were made to thrive.

Those at the mastermind meeting didn't know that success was right around the corner. They didn't know they'd get to sit in a meeting and share their wins.

All they knew was that they wanted more and took action to get it.

What do you want to have changed a year from now in your life?

Claim your free gift!

GET THE BEHIND THE CURTAIN POWER PACK

Claim over $10,358 worth of bonuses, including:

- Million Dollar Swipe file by Kim Walsh Phillips
- It's My Birthday Credit Promo by Dr. Russell Strickland
- Ultimate Relaxation recording by Jennifer Carman
- Graphics Branding Tutorial Video, Social Media Clever Caption Guide, and Social Media Timing Cheat Sheet by Mimi Sheffer
- 14 Days Without Sugar guide by Magda Castañeda
- A review of your current phone answering and follow-up process (or create one from scratch) and work one on one to customize your process with Howard Globus
- "4 Easy Steps To Fit Into Your Skinny Jeans" digital book by Cathy Frost
- The Course Creator SuperBundle by Suzi Seddon
- The Ultimate Secure Retirement Roadmap by Dr. Fred Rouse
- $1199 worth of savings and promotions from FASTSIGNS
- 27 Headline Formulas Guaranteed to Convert by Denise Fay
- And much, much more besides!

BEHINDTHESCENESBOOK.COM/POWERPACK

KIM WALSH PHILLIPS

KIM WALSH PHILLIPS is the founder of Powerful Professionals, a business coaching and education company. She was recently named #475 in the Inc 5000 and is a multi-seven-figure business entrepreneur with no business degree and a tendency to say "crazy pants" more than is socially acceptable. She is the best-selling author of *The Ultimate Guide to Instagram for Business* and *The No BS Guide To Direct Response Social Media Marketing*. (Fun fact: she uses a thesaurus when she writes or she would use the words "awesome," "cool," and "very" 7,452,675 more times than she already does.)

She's an in-demand speaker, having shared the stage with Tony Robbins, Grant Cardone, Kevin O'Leary, and Gary Vaynerchuk.

She's a Boss. A mom. A wife. A daughter. A friend. And knows that's why God gave us prayer, laughter, and coffee.

@TheKimWalshPhillips

Made in the USA
Monee, IL
23 October 2020

45902429R00134